10 THINGS GIRLS NEED MOST

10 THINGS GIRLS NEED MOST

NEED MOST

to grow up strong and free

STEVE BIDDULPH

Thorsons

Thorsons
An imprint of HarperCollins*Publishers*
1 London Bridge Street
London SE1 9GF

www.harpercollins.co.uk

First published by Thorsons 2017

10 9 8 7 6 5 4 3 2 1

Design: Bobby&Co Book Design

A catalogue record of this book is available from
the British Library

ISBN 978-0-00-814679-5

Printed and bound in China

The information, ideas and exercises in this book are intended to help
discussion and reflection only. You should use your own judgement,
knowledge of your own child and, if need be, seek professional help with
any concerns for their wellbeing.

Stories of girls, their parents and their schools in this book are composited
and identifying details are altered to maintain privacy.

MIX
Paper from
responsible sources
FSC® C007454

FSC™ is a non-profit international organisation established to promote the
responsible management of the world's forests. Products carrying the FSC
label are independently certified to assure consumers that they come from
forests that are managed to meet the social, economic and ecological needs
of present and future generations, and other controlled sources.

Find out more about HarperCollins and the environment at
www.harpercollins.co.uk/green

Also by Steve Biddulph

Raising Boys
Raising Girls
Raising Babies
The New Manhood

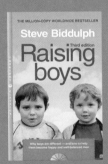  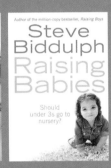 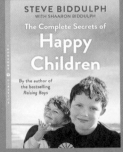

with Shaaron Biddulph

The Secret of Happy Parents
The Complete Secrets of Happy Children
Love, Laughter and Parenting

Contents

10 THINGS GIRLS NEED MOST

A letter from Steve

Dear Reader

For forty years I've worked with parents in groups, and it is so satisfying, and so moving, that I wanted to share that with everyone in the world. So I set about thinking how to bring the same experience to you in a book. What you hold in your hands is the result. You can read it straight through, like any other book, but – if you wish to go further – on every few pages there are opportunities to interact. These are very simple – a self-evaluation quiz, or an idea to give a quick rating to. These instant response items get you personalizing the ideas and applying them to your own life, your family, and especially your daughter.

We have field-tested these sections, and found that parents love the sudden flashes of insight they can bring. And they're fun! You will find yourself seeing more clearly and understanding things that previously had you totally baffled or lost. And, from this, you will become more the parent your daughter needs you to be.

So, please – read these pages with a pen handy. Give it a try and see. (Many of us, when we were little, would have got into trouble for scribbling in a book. I hope you will get over that!) You can download the questionnaires at www.stevebiddulph.co.uk/resources.

One more thing – it sometimes happens that the questions can bring tears, or other strong emotions, and I hope you will sense on these pages the support and care of others going through the very same things. We have to take care of each other in this journey to make the world better for all our girls.

Much love,

Steve

You can also use this book as a discussion guide with your friends. Taking one chapter at a time, you can create your own ongoing support group to help you care for all your daughters together. That's how girls were meant to be raised — by a tribe.

Foreword

THE BATTLE TO SET GIRLS FREE

You remember that moment, don't you? Holding your baby daughter in your arms for the very first time. Her eyes wide open, gazing back into yours. Feeling so protective, so proud, so happy. A daughter!

Throughout the last hundred years, things have got better for girls. People fought hard for our daughters to have more equality and opportunity and to be less pushed into narrow boxes of what a girl, or woman, could be. But about ten years ago – it's hard to say just when – all this started to change. Girls who had flown up in the sunshine of a century of feminism started to go into a nosedive.

Everyone has noticed this – not just psychologists and counsellors, but parents themselves. They say, 'Fourteen is the new eighteen,' or 'They're growing up too fast.' Or they just roll their eyes and say, 'Girls!'

As I am writing this, the Department for Education is reporting that a third of all teenage girls in the UK suffer from depression or anxiety. They are calling it 'an important and significant trend'. The NHS says the same; they report that 20 per cent of girls are self-harming – three times as many as ten years ago. Not only that; 13 per cent of girls have symptoms of post-traumatic stress – something we associate with serious trauma or harm. Eating disorders, body-hate, having unhappy and unwanted sex: all are on the increase. It's not all girls, but it's enough of them to worry about.

We know the causes of this change in girlhood. It's partly the explosion of social media and the amount of time we spend on screens, but also the pressured and competitive way we live today. The disappearance of spending time with older, wiser, kinder people in the real world, as well as time in nature, being playful in a relaxed, dreamy way that is best for growing young brains.

We know what is needed to help a girl grow up strong and free, and it's not what television, the internet, magazines or billboards are telling her. It's also not testing in primary school. Nor it is looks, being hot, being cool, pleasing boys or fitting in to tidy models of corporate success (unless that's really what she wants!).

So here, from the front line of working with girls and their parents, are the ten things that girls need most. This book works by building self-awareness, clarity and purpose. By enlivening your own parenting instincts. By giving you the best information, then letting YOU choose what to do for YOUR girl, and her friends, and your nieces, granddaughters or students.

It's a mighty kit bag of tools for liberating your girl. You might even free yourself along the way. After all, we could all do with some liberation.

This is an interactive book. So here is your first go – what is your gut reaction right now?

(Tick which statement is the closest to how you feel.)

☐   **1.**   Hell no, I don't want to know! Hide me from all this.

☐   **2.**   I'm nervous, but I will read on. I love my daughter and want to help her.

☐   **3.**   I am stirred up already and want to get kicking. Let me loose!

YOUR DAUGHTER'S JOURNEY

Your daughter is unique. There is no-one like her in the whole world. And she has a unique reason for being here, a purpose to discover and unfold in her life. Your part in this is huge, and it all begins with appreciating her. Seeing her more deeply than anyone else, and loving what you see. Nurturing what is good, and getting to work on what needs to be strengthened.

This self-evaluation will help you to get clear about two things. Firstly – the girl she is now. And secondly – the woman she will become – with your help. It's a beautiful exercise to do. So, let's start…

1. I have _____ daughter/s.

If you have more than one daughter, choose one girl to focus on during each exercise throughout the book, then return and do the others later.

2. Her age is:

0 1 2 3 4 5 6 7 8 9 10 11 12 13 14 15 16 17 18 19 20 21 older? _____

3. Her name is:

_____

_____

_____

_____

The Girl She Is Now
Three things I like and admire most about her are:

1. _____

2. _____

3. _____

What I notice is changing the most about her is:

_____

What I want to give her the most is:

_____

What I think she gives me the most is:

_____

The Woman She Will Become

Now that you have a clear view of your girl, it's time to look to the _destination_.
The woman you want her to become.

Imagine your daughter when she is twenty-five years old.
Imagine that she has turned out as you would have hoped in your heart that she would.

What three qualities do you hope that she will have, that people will see
in her, or experience in her?

1. _____

2. _____

3. _____

What do you notice when you compare the 'hoped-for qualities'
and the ones she already has?

_____

_____

_____

Your daughter is unique. There is no-one
else like her in the whole world.

WHERE IS SHE NOW?

Now you have focused on what your daughter
is like and the goals you have for her, we can get
started on helping those goals come true. We can
find out exactly where she is on the journey. This
will help you to know what is needed right now.

As parents, we know that our mission is not just
about getting kids fed, washed, off to school and
having fun on weekends. We also know that it's
going somewhere. Every day, little by little, your
daughter is moving closer to womanhood. There is
a journey that she is on, and you are her guide. So
you need to have a map.

In my book *Raising Girls*, I set out a map of the
major stages of girlhood. These stages are now used
by thousands of parents around the world. These
are simple and you will recognize them if you think
about the girls you know.

Zero to two, two to five, five to ten, ten to
fourteen, and fourteen to eighteen are each a
distinctive stage based on what is the main thing
going on at that age. (Of course, they overlap, and
the timing varies from child to child – but not a lot!)
The stages help you to know what to concentrate
on, what matters most.

In the overwhelming time of parenthood, you
can easily lose the wood for the trees, the baby with
the bathwater, or the teenager behind the temper.
The stages help you stay on track.

Here is each stage with its main lesson. Or put
another way, the single most important thing to
focus on at her age:

0–2   Is she loved and SECURE?

2–5   Does she feel confident and encouraged
to EXPLORE the world and enjoy it?

5–10   Has she got the skills to make FRIENDS,
have fun, and get along with people in
general?

10–14 Who is she, as a UNIQUE person –
what are her values and beliefs?

14–18 Is she PREPARED and trained, practically,
to enter adult life?

The existence of these stages are something
parents learn from experience. For example, if a
friend asked you to mind their two-year-old for a
day, you could expect a busy time. The day might
be fun, but not exactly serene. If a fourteen-year-
old was joining you for dinner, you might expect a
certain awkwardness, mixed with moments of pure
delight. The stages are universal, and timeless. And
fortunately, we know how to make them go well.

THE QUEST OF GIRLHOOD

There is a beautiful and accurate way of looking at girlhood. It is a 'quest' – a journey with a purpose, a path along which she gathers the ingredients of her womanhood. We are her main guides, especially early on, and always there in the background later, just helping it go more easily. In raising a child we always have this dual awareness. We enjoy each day for its own sake. But we also have in our mind the big picture – what is important for her to experience and learn in preparation for the time when *we* are no longer there to help her.

Knowing the stages is incredibly helpful, because it keeps us to a plan. Our goal is making a wonderful woman. And that's what the stages do.

So – we start with a simple question.

What age is your daughter right now?

Now the important question – since she may have passed through a number of stages, see if you can rate how well they were achieved, in your opinion, using the scoresheet opposite.

Do this off the cuff, even if you don't fully understand what the stages mean yet. We'll return to them in detail later, but this is a starting point.

I've inverted the stages so you can see them as a kind of building, with foundations at the bottom. (If your daughter is under two, you can only rank the bottom line. If she is aged from two to five you can rate the second item as well. If she is aged from five to ten the third, ten to fourteen the fourth. and fourteen and over, the fifth. So you have rated all the way up to the age she is.)

Give each life-stage from one to five stars, just as if you were rating a hotel. ⭐

5. Trained for adulthood   ☐ ☐ ☐ ☐ ☐   14–18 years

4. Found her own self   ☐ ☐ ☐ ☐ ☐   10–14 years

3. Good at friendship   ☐ ☐ ☐ ☐ ☐   5–10 years

2. Confident to explore   ☐ ☐ ☐ ☐ ☐   2–5 years

1. Loved and secure   ☐ ☐ ☐ ☐ ☐   0–2 years

Can you see where the gaps are?

Where might she need your help to repair missing or weak stages in her growing up? The neuroplasticity of the human brain means it's usually possible to put in experiences that were missed the first time around. (The chapters to come will help you to do this.)

Complete this sentence

'I think we need to work to improve stage _____'

HOW ABOUT YOU?

And now the really profound question – and perhaps the most useful. If you are her mum – how well did those stages go in your own growing up years? If you are her dad – same question.

Slow right down now to think about this. It's going to be a bit sobering for some readers, because our own childhoods might have been disastrous. That's why we are so motivated to do better for our girls than was done for us.

If you can identify the stages you had trouble with, or times when you did not have your needs met very well, then you will be much more aware and able to get it right with your own girl. This might be the most important thing you do in this whole book.

Mum's Girlhood Profile

In your own girlhood, how well were these needs met? Give each a rating from one to five stars. Start at the bottom (no. 1) and work your way up.

5. 14–18 Trained for adulthood   ☐ ☐ ☐ ☐ ☐

4. 10–14 Found her own self   ☐ ☐ ☐ ☐ ☐

3. 5–10 Good with friends   ☐ ☐ ☐ ☐ ☐

2. 2–5 Confident to explore   ☐ ☐ ☐ ☐ ☐

1. 0–2 Loved and secure   ☐ ☐ ☐ ☐ ☐

This can be important when your daughter is going through a stage that was not easy or well cared for during your own growing up. That means getting some extra support to make sure you can help her in the very best way you can. Don't worry, there is a lot more in this book about how to do that. You are awake now to the challenge and it's certainly going to go better because of that.

Dad's Boyhood Profile

(Or Co-parent if you are a same-sex couple)

While boyhood has a different set of stages and ages to girls, we have kept things simple by just using the same ones. It will still work as a guide. In your childhood, how well were these needs met? Award up to five stars for each point

5. 14–18 Trained for adulthood   ☐ ☐ ☐ ☐ ☐

4. 10–14 Found his own self   ☐ ☐ ☐ ☐ ☐

3. 5–10 Good with friends   ☐ ☐ ☐ ☐ ☐

2. 2–5 Confident to explore   ☐ ☐ ☐ ☐ ☐

1. 0–2 Loved and secure   ☐ ☐ ☐ ☐ ☐

ADVANCED EXERCISE

If you are a couple, you might want to try this.
Add the scores of your two profiles together.
So each row will have a score out of ten.

Combined Mum and Dad (or Partner) Profile

5. Trained for adulthood   ☐ ☐ ☐ ☐ ☐ ☐ ☐ ☐ ☐ ☐

4. Found their own self   ☐ ☐ ☐ ☐ ☐ ☐ ☐ ☐ ☐ ☐

3. Good with friends   ☐ ☐ ☐ ☐ ☐ ☐ ☐ ☐ ☐ ☐

2. Confident to explore   ☐ ☐ ☐ ☐ ☐ ☐ ☐ ☐ ☐ ☐

1. Loved and secure   ☐ ☐ ☐ ☐ ☐ ☐ ☐ ☐ ☐ ☐

If you look at the profile for both of you added together, you might find that you fill in each other's gaps in a very helpful way. Or not! This is the psychology of your family when combining your strengths and weaknesses. It tells you what you have to work on developing. As long as you have a minimum of six stars – between you – on each stage, then you can probably relax about those stages. If one or more stages look a bit wobbly, then this book, as you go through it, will help you with these.

Our family needs to focus most on the _____ stage.

Be of good cheer! It's easier to overcome any gaps if you know what they are. In family life, it's the things you don't know about yourselves – the blind spots we all have – that cause the biggest problems. Once you see clearly, you have much more power to make changes. Once you know, you are set to give your daughter what she needs (even if you didn't get it yourself).

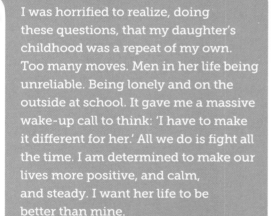

I was horrified to realize, doing these questions, that my daughter's childhood was a repeat of my own. Too many moves. Men in her life being unreliable. Being lonely and on the outside at school. It gave me a massive wake-up call to think: 'I have to make it different for her.' All we do is fight all the time. I am determined to make our lives more positive, and calm, and steady. I want her life to be better than mine.

Lorna, 42

It all came down to stress. We were financially secure but just too hurried and hassled. In my childhood we had been poor immigrants, and my parents very busy, but in the here and now, we didn't need to be so wound up. The questions made me see that we had work to do to make life more happy and focused on everyday moments. It didn't have to be the struggle that my childhood was.

Damien, 31

Now, we know exactly where your daughter is. It's time to begin the main part of the book. **The Ten Things Girls Need Most**…

10 THINGS GIRLS NEED MOST

Chapter One

A
Secure
and
Loving
Start

> " It all begins in your arms.
> Her knowing that she is cherished and
> safe. But to give her that security, we have
> to be in the right place ourselves. "

This chapter is about how to get the most important thing about childhood right. That is, to help your daughter have a deep-down feeling of security and worth. Everyone alive needs to have this, because it helps us to feel at ease in the world, able to be close to others, and able to relax. Babyhood is the best time to get this feeling, but it's never too late to start.

For a little child, mum and dad are her whole world. Their emotions are her emotions. A baby doesn't know (or care) if she lives in a tin shed or a palace, as long as those caring for her are kind and peaceful. If we can manage that, at least some of the time, then long after we are gone she will carry this memory inside her. When times are hard, it will be there for her to draw on. Of course, this can be hard for us to hear, because our adult world is a rushed and stressful place. We might have spent our lives racing to get ahead. But with a baby or toddler, the priorities are changed. The most valuable thing we can do is – very little. We need to calm things down.

Imagine for a moment what it would feel like to be a small baby, with someone's arms holding you gently and a loving face looking down at you. See if you can feel in your body what that would be like, and enjoy it for a moment. Imagine knowing that you are at the very centre of this person's love and concern. Knowing that they will capably and caringly look after you. That you have no need to do anything, prove anything or fear anything. That they delight in you, and enjoy you, and love you and will give you all that you need. That you are totally safe. Just imagine all these things, and notice how that feels in your body. Where do you feel it? What is it like?

THIS IS THE FEELING WE WANT OUR CHILDREN TO START OFF WITH

This kind of experience for your daughter can only come from having you, her parent/s – and hopefully a handful of other people as well – who love her and actively show that. This is best and most easily done when she is a baby, but it carries all the way through. And if you're reading this because you have a ten-year-old or a seventeen-year-old then it's still fine – you can still fix this. You'll find out how, as this book goes on.

HOW TO MAKE SURE
SHE'S SECURE

'Am I loved and secure?' That question is at the heart of every whimper she makes, every gaze she sends out in search of your smile, every excursion she makes crawling or toddling across the grass or the floor before scurrying back to your arms.

It's a huge question. It depends on a mother (or father or other carer) being safe themselves. Supported. Not stressed by outside factors. It depends on those around the mother – a partner, grandparents, neighbours and friends – being caring and warm to her, so she can do the same for her baby. It depends on her having memories of warmth and security in her own life, if not in babyhood then at some later time.

Babies need to be loved for a very practical reason, because that means they will be attended to, fed, soothed, kept clean and safe, talked to and sung to and played with. That takes time – huge amounts of it. And it takes an adult sufficiently mature in themselves to put this little creature's needs ahead of their own. Love isn't just a gooey feeling, it's a blazing fire, a massive power source to carry you through all these things. That's why it has to be kindled well.

So, here is a rating for your situation during your daughter's early years – give each point a rating out of five stars (5 is VERY, 1 is HARDLY AT ALL). Go slowly with this, and really think it over. When your daughter was under two:

1. How relaxed was your life?

2. How supportive was your partner?

3. How materially secure did you feel (housing, money, health care)?

4. How supportive were others – grandparents, neighbours, friends?

5. Did you bring to this task a calm, settled nature, or were you naturally nervous, jumpy or anxious (circle one)?

very nervous and afraid   1   2   3   4   5   so calm I almost fell asleep

These questions add up to the whole picture, and so total your scores. **My total** _____

If you have less than 10, that's quite a stressful time. Around 15 would be about average – not too bad. Over 20 would be a miracle!

For many reading this, the scoring on the previous page will come as a bit of a blow, because parenthood in the modern world has been made terribly stressful, and unsupported. We may be materially very secure, but emotionally far from that. Or the reverse. Or neither.

And there is another option. It's possible the questionnaire is completely wrong in your case. Sometimes that can happen. You can have had a terrible time in the first year, little support, poor circumstances materially, isolated from others, and awful childhood memories of your own, and yet by sheer fierceness of your love and commitment, you just made sure her situation was nurturing, responsive and calm. Draw a circle around this sentence, just to celebrate...

> **'I think I have overcome tough circumstances, or a terrible background of my own, and still made sure my daughter felt loved.'**

Massive admiration and love to you.

And if not, if either way you look at it, it wasn't an ideal start – don't blame yourself. Don't blame others. Allow that there may have been a stress burden, in your family and in your daughter's early experience, which may explain some of the challenges she has. There are things you can do about these, but it begins with an honest appraisal.

If the sense of being loved and secure is wobbly, then that has to be the primary focus. Even if she is ten or sixteen, repairing those babyhood feelings might still be the priority. She might really need lots of cuddles and quiet times with you each day just to settle down her autonomic nervous system which has always been set on 'red alert' since she was little. She can be capable, helpful, and deal with the big world, but still need to stop and fill her tank regularly until her mind learns that she really is secure.

> Our daughter was adopted: she came to live with us when she was one. We don't even know what her babyhood was like – we suspect it was pretty terrible. She had quite a lot of issues growing up. But we loved her relentlessly and patiently, and knew she needed lots of reassurance, routine, lots of cuddles, lots of building up. We had read in Steve's books that at the age of thirteen children 'recycle' their babyhood, or have a second babyhood, that makes them more open to love and affection. So we babied her a lot at that age. By fourteen she was completely out of that stage, and she has been going great ever since. She'll always be a rather intense girl, I think, but her life is going fine.
>
> *Mark, 48 and Amy, 42*

> When my baby was one, I had to leave China for a year to study in the US. Our baby stayed with her grandma. When I came home, it was to have a second new baby. So our relationship is quite wobbly. She was fine with her grandma, but can't live with her now. I am not sure that my career path has been good for her, and hope I can make it up to her.
>
> *Guan-yin, 38*

Loving small children is natural – we have hormones like oxytocin which help us to feel melty and soft when we are around them. But that doesn't mean that the caring role comes naturally to everyone, because though the feeling may be there, the doing of it has to be learned. If we haven't seen or experienced how loving is done, we might actually be quite tense and awkward in expressing our love for our baby. (Sometimes a mother or father feels almost nothing at all towards their new baby, and has to start gradually by getting to know them, and being helped with outside support to do this.) Almost everyone today has gaps in their ability to love, but don't worry about this because, rather like a fire, you can create and kindle the beginnings and it starts to take off by itself.

There are two things that increase the capacity for love in your family. These love sources are:

1. Slowing down your world.

2. Getting into the river of love.

Let's explain what these mean...

Slowing Down

THE SECRET OF WHERE LOVE GROWS

When I talk to audiences of parents, I watch and listen closely. Some ideas make people go quiet. Some make them laugh out loud. Some make the room light up with acknowledgement – of 'Yes, that's right!'. A good example of that last one is that HURRY IS THE ENEMY OF LOVE. When we are rushing through our lives, our interactions get more and more jarring and unsatisfying, even insensitive. The warmth and harmony between us disappears. Husbands and wives stop getting along. Parents and children annoy and irritate each other. Love is there, but it's eaten away by not quite being attuned to each other, and so things go badly. Reaffirming closeness, understanding 'where each other is at', takes time. If you have children, especially small ones, then slowness is essential to love being able to grow.

For love to exist between a parent and child (or adult and adult) they have to first feel settled and present. You have to be tuned in – to yourself, and to them.

The sequence for making human connection is timeless. It can only go in this order. You settle down. You breathe and your shoulders relax and you sink into the chair. You begin to feel at home inside yourself. (Sometimes you realize – 'I am really hungry', or 'I need a wee!' It might be good to fix this!) Now, there is this baby, or toddler, or older child in front of you. From your feeling of OK-ness in yourself, you reach out to them. Perhaps they are fretting and anxious, or needy, or wanting to talk to you or get your help. Because you are OK on the inside, and have the time, their distress doesn't distress you. You care about them, and are happy to help.

So you soothe them with words or touch, and they feel that you are calm, so they start to calm down too. (Babies and toddlers can't regulate their own emotions. Many times a day, a baby or small child will 'freak out' at something strange, a loud noise, a stranger, falling and hurting themselves, a frustration they encounter, not getting what they want, or just some reason you or they can't even figure out. A lot of what we do as parents is soothing these reactions, just holding them patiently as they let those feelings abate, and letting them settle, so they find a way out of their distress. After several years of us providing this, the pathways in their mind to a calmer state will be well trodden, and they will be able to do this for themselves.) If your child is old enough to talk, of course it's easier: you listen to their worries, or help in a practical way, but you still keep that calm sense of attention and patience. They feel loved and noticed. They don't need to be naughty or difficult to get your attention.

But this means you must not be busy! Which is tough, because the big world wants you to rush – timetables, bills, appointments, lessons and meals are all crowding in. It wants you to earn money, spend money, buy stuff you don't need, be always on the go with self-improving activities, rushing kids to classes and sports and so on. Life is just so complicated and full – how can we do it without rush? And yet, when we rush, things always go wrong. Have you noticed that?

> I noticed something about myself – that I had a hurried feeling on the inside nearly all the time. It occurred to me – could I do things, even busy things, and be very active, but have a peaceful inside as I was doing it? Gradually I realized that I could. It meant being really mindful, and cultivating that feeling. You can be fast, but peaceful, for short bursts at least. You have to stop making yourself all stressy, stop being in the victim position. It's rather good to enjoy getting a lot done while feeling good on the inside. But I still prefer lying around when I can!
>
> *Serena, 40*

So here is a very important first question.

Am I too busy?
(Tick which statement fits you best.)

☐   **1.** Yes, but I have to be to survive.

☐   **2.** Yes, and I want to do something about it.

☐   **3.** Sometimes things get crazy, but generally it calms down again.

☐   **4.** Changes have been made. I'm currently living at a slower pace than previously and it's so much better now.

How Love Grows

To sum up – love takes time. It's rare for two human beings to love each other from the very first moment. Even with little babies. Love is an interchange – you give a little, get something back, give more, get more back. This has to be tentative, respectful, you have to get attuned to each other. And even though we love each other, that connection is a living thing – it has to be re-established whenever we meet. It's the same between husband and wife at the end of the day, or parent and a child who has been away all day at school.

In the way that families live now, though, hurrying can mean that this quality of connection happens less and less. Before long, you are just people under the same roof, living separate lives. Almost every marriage drifts into this place sometimes, and it's lonely and sad. You have to win back the time, whatever it costs. It's cheaper than divorce, or a child seeing a psychiatrist, or a teenager on drugs. (Drug use among teenagers does not correlate with any specific factor, such as poverty, but it does correlate with lack of parental time.) Sometimes you have to 'put your family back together' by slowing it down. Rekindle the respect and caring in your relationships. Rebond with the teenagers who all you seem to do is 'manage'. Resteady your school-aged child who has become overscheduled. And settle your new baby by just hanging out with them for long lazy times. Win back the time of your life and use it to make your family harmonious again.

Have you ever done this deliberate slowing down of life?

Do you think this is needed in your family at the moment?

It might need the help of others in your family to achieve this. Talk it over. Make practical decisions about what might have to be dropped or let go, to reduce the hurry and rush.

The River of Love

Sometimes it isn't possible to create love out of nowhere. There is a shortage – everyone in the family is running on an empty tank. How can you fill each other up? If your life is feeling impossible, then there is something else you have to do. You have to get into the 'river'.

We humans are a species that developed with strong social supports always surrounding us. For millions of years our ancestors lived in caring, supportive groups, large extended families or clans of twenty to forty people. So when we start a family, it's quite urgent that we seek out the 'village' that we are going to need. Nothing is more important for parents than to receive love and care themselves, so that they can give it to their child.

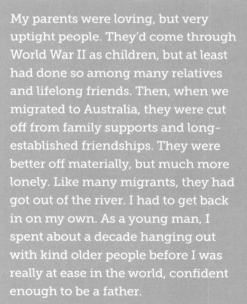

> My parents were loving, but very uptight people. They'd come through World War II as children, but at least had done so among many relatives and lifelong friends. Then, when we migrated to Australia, they were cut off from family supports and long-established friendships. They were better off materially, but much more lonely. Like many migrants, they had got out of the river. I had to get back in on my own. As a young man, I spent about a decade hanging out with kind older people before I was really at ease in the world, confident enough to be a father.
>
> *Will, 62*

You must, if you are a parent, and especially if you are finding it hard, seek out kind people to talk to, hang around with, get encouragement from. I remember as a young dad, just having to go to a playground and talk to the first other parent who came along. But sometimes it needs someone older, less competing or judgemental. In your neighbourhood, workplace, or in more formal ways like counselling or parenting groups and courses, find people who are loving and learn from them. Accept their care and attention as a necessary part of your parental role.

How would you describe your own sociability at this time in your life? (Tick the one that comes closest.)

☐ **1.** I am a lone wolf. Nobody knows me, or cares about me.

☐ **2.** I am a reluctant lone wolf. I would like more emotional support, but don't know where to find it.

☐ **3.** I am starting to reach out, make friends and get help from supportive people.

☐ **4.** I am connecting with other people a lot now, and it's really helping.

☐ **5.** I am well-nourished emotionally, and now enjoy being a support to younger parents or others. I am passing on what I received, and it's a joy to do.

Who is there, in your world, that could give you more support and comfort, encouragement and help?

_____

_____

_____

Could you let them know you need that?

How would it go?

What would it take to get a more supportive network around you?

Or even just one friendly face that you regularly can count on?

If you are an older parent, are there young parents in your world who could use some help or encouragement?

How could you do that?

By doing these two things – having more time, and finding people who can be kind to you and getting their help – the first two years of your daughter's life will go so much better. And at any age from two to adult, doing this can help repair or strengthen what you have to give her, and the bond between you that results.

> I was the ultimate loner. We moved from place to place. I didn't trust other people. I wasn't good at making friends, and once or twice I tried and was badly taken advantage of. But having a baby I realized I just had to, and luckily other parents I have met have been just great. Kids are a great excuse for making friends.
>
> *Donna, 22*

WHAT IF WE MISSED THIS STAGE?

Perhaps you have older children, but you noticed when you filled in the profile of your daughter's girlhood at the beginning of the book that she did not rate very well on this stage? Don't fret! The great thing about children and teenagers is that they give you many chances. If a stage has not been fulfilled, they unconsciously know that, and will show signs that they want something from you. It might not be obvious – often naughtiness or arguing or having problems in the big world are the language they use to say 'notice me'. Here are some clues to what you can do.

In *The Secrets of Happy Children* (both the book and the talks I give) we explain how, around the age of twelve, kids start a second babyhood. This is caused by the neurological meltdown or pruning phase in the brain that marks the start of adolescence and puberty. (Brain puberty does not always occur the same as the physical signs of puberty. Breast development can now come much sooner due to environmental influences. Brain puberty is still usually around the age of twelve.)

The effect of puberty on the brain is so great that a teenager recycles right through the stages of growing up, between twelve and eighteen (and longer with boys). The great thing about this is that you get a second chance to get these stages right. As a rough guide, if you subtract twelve from your daughter's age, you will pinpoint what age she is going through for the second time. So many thirteen-year-olds are like babies – confused, a bit lost, but also very emotionally open. You can rebond with a thirteen-year-old, cuddle them, feed them and comfort them, and they will let you!

Fourteen-year-olds go through another 'terrible twos' stage, and so you will need to keep your sense of humour, but also hold firm on boundaries, and not let them get you riled into shouting or making threats you can't keep (special dad alert here).

In spite of their actual age in years, many children stay stuck at the stage where they didn't get what they needed. They wait there until we are able to figure out and provide the missing experiences. The great thing about this is that we get a second chance (and a third and a fourth and so on). We can get in and repair the holes. A timid child can be gradually encouraged to be more adventurous, and see the fun in it, and loosen up and be messy and loud. A child who didn't learn friendship can talk about that with you, and make strategies and learn to be social. And an insecure child can begin to trust and relax. We can always fix the past if we are logical and a little bit brave. There's a lot more about this in the chapters still to come.

Many children stay stuck at the stage where they didn't get what they needed.

A
Secure
and
Loving
Start

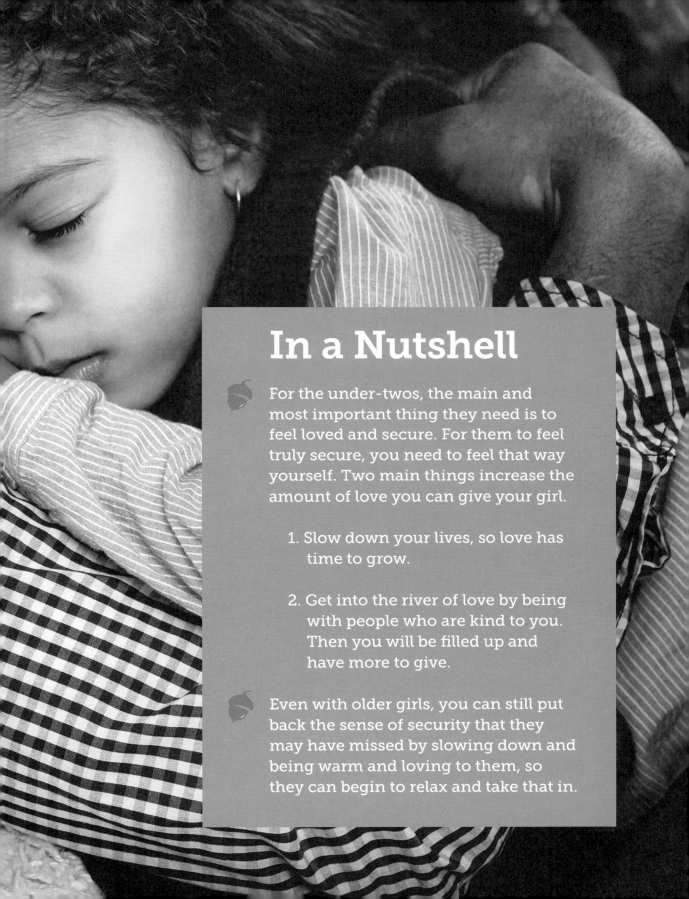

In a Nutshell

For the under-twos, the main and most important thing they need is to feel loved and secure. For them to feel truly secure, you need to feel that way yourself. Two main things increase the amount of love you can give your girl.

1. Slow down your lives, so love has time to grow.

2. Get into the river of love by being with people who are kind to you. Then you will be filled up and have more to give.

Even with older girls, you can still put back the sense of security that they may have missed by slowing down and being warm and loving to them, so they can begin to relax and take that in.

Chapter Two

The Chance to be Wild and Time to be a Child

" Even as young as two, the world puts limits onto girls. We have to encourage our daughters to be adventurous and brave, to help them stay in touch with their wild nature. And we have to fight the forces that want to steal their childhood away. "

Get a group of parents together anywhere in the world today, and start them talking about girls. Within three minutes I guarantee you will hear these words: *'They are growing up too fast.'*

These parents aren't talking about the age-old feeling that our children are up and gone before we know it, but something new and much more concerning. In just one generation, many childhoods have been snapped in half by new forces, unprecedented in history. Effectively, girls have lost four or more years of childhood. You will see the effects of this everywhere you go – 'adultified' girls of twelve or thirteen with cleavages self-consciously displayed and faces covered in make-up, dressed to kill (possibly from pneumonia), stressing out over how boys might judge them. And being neither happy nor free.

Mothers and fathers everywhere say that 'fourteen is the new eighteen'. And given what we know about the massive changes in the brain in those four years, and all the learning that takes place – how very different we are at eighteen from fourteen – *that has to be a problem.*

Think back to your own teenage years. At eighteen you were starting to make choices about sex, drugs and alcohol, your own safety, and so on, which were complex and difficult. You were dealing for the first time with unpleasant or unscrupulous people, outside the safe circles of family and friends. And you were finding it a challenge. Even at eighteen, being eighteen is hard. But at fourteen (or these days, more often, twelve) girls are so ill-equipped – unpractised in separating emotion

from thought, their confidence based entirely on bluff, their brains still not properly formed. They will struggle to deal with these choices, and so, increasingly, their lives may fall apart at this vulnerable age.

Let's be clear – most girls still turn out fine. We help them, support them and arm them against the excesses of the culture, and they turn into wonderful strong women. Three out of five girls still do this. But one in five does not. They go so far off the rails that their adult life is really impaired.

Another one in five goes through some sort of a crisis, which galvanizes their family to action, and they pull through. But that still means way too many girls having way too hard a time.

A girl needs to be strong. Where that comes from is being tuned into her own nature, trusting her feelings and instincts. Having physical confidence. And growing slowly, getting all her abilities – mental and physical – unfolding as they were intended to through millions of years of human development. And it's very early on – in the years from two to five – that we can make the most difference to her resilience. This is where we can sow the seeds of a girl who enjoys being the age she is, and isn't rushed into fake grown-upness. If you grow slow, you grow strong.

HOW FREE AND WILD WERE YOU?

For younger mothers and fathers aged in their late twenties and thirties, some of these changes were already starting in your own childhood. We are not assuming here that the past was good. It's important to look at what you bring to this stage from your own background.

Can you remember the time in your childhood when you were most happy and free?

What age was that?

1   2   3   4   5   6   7   8   9   10   11   12   13   14   15   16   17   18

What was great about it?

_____

_____

_____

What did other people do, if anything, to make it possible?

_____

_____

_____

Was there a time in your childhood when you felt you were NOT happy and free? What age was that?

1   2   3   4   5   6   7   8   9   10   11   12   13   14   15   16   17   18

What happened to make you feel that way?

_____

_____

_____

_____

What could others have done, that they did not do, to have helped you at that time?

_____

_____

_____

_____

It may be that this has reminded you of sad or hard times in your life. Breathe deep and notice that this was a long time ago. You are here now. Well done for having got through those times and becoming a loving and involved mother or father, wanting to do it better for your own girl or girls. Or it may be that you realized people really did pretty well in raising you. And you appreciate that more.

There is nothing better to help us be a sensitive parent than remembering what our own childhood was like. If you do that, you will know so much more about how to be the mother or father your daughter needs.

KEEPING HER FREE

It's important to think about how great girlhood can be, and not settle for less. Girlhood – before puberty comes along – can be a wonderful time of life. Unworried by concerns about the opposite sex – or totally dismissive of them – free in her body, bold in her actions, able to be creative without fearing judgement, loving the world of animals and nature, affectionate with friends of both sexes, enjoying her parents' company. How we wish this time would last for ever. *And there is no reason why it shouldn't.*

But we parents have to do two things to make sure this is the case. First, we have to encourage and nurture her exploratory and wild self, so that it grows strong and lasts all her life. And second, we have to fence out the toxic messages that have sprung up around girls in recent years. This means we have to be choosy about what media we bring or let into our own home and even think about how our own attitudes can affect her without us knowing it. (For often the problems girls have also affected their mothers first.) Only by doing both these things – 'powering up' and 'fencing out', can we create the conditions for a strong happy woman to grow.

The age range from two to five is where this needs to begin. But you can work to correct this at any age. Remember when you filled in the profile of your daughter's girlhood back at the start of the book? If you rated this second stage – exploration – at three stars or less, then there is plenty you can do at eight or fourteen or even later to help her bring her strong, 'wild' self to life.

In fact you may need to do some remedial 'rewilding' of yourself to be really happy as a mum or dad, and pass on this permission to your daughter as well.

So let's make a baseline assessment of how exploratory, adventure-loving and confident your daughter is. You'll notice we've combined two kinds of adventurousness – outwards, physically, in the world, and inwards in creativity and mental freedom. Of course, having both is brilliant.

Tick which of these best describes your girl:

☐　**1.** She is very anxious, neat and buttoned up. She is happiest playing with an iPad as it doesn't mess up her clothes.

☐　**2.** She sometimes does creative or adventurous things. But not a lot.

☐　**3.** She loves to play, outdoors or inside: she gets noisy, makes a bit of a mess and loves having adventures.

☐　**4.** We haven't seen her for three days, but she sends a smoke signal from a ridge at sunset, so we know she's OK.

Now, role modelling has to come into this. So we have to ask a second question:

How about you when you were a child?

☐　**1.** I was very anxious, neat and buttoned up. I did embroidery, but only between the lines.

☐　**2.** I did occasionally do something creative or adventurous. But it got me into trouble.

☐　**3.** I loved to play, get noisy and make a bit of a mess, and had many adventures.

☐　**4.** I hitchhiked across the country at seven, and wrote a book about it called *Truck Drivers Are My Friends*.

(Please note, this is not to say that every girl, or boy, should be loud and highly active. Some kids are naturally quieter and more into fine motor activity which is just great. The question is: do they feel free. Are their spirits soaring, or afraid?)

The years from two to five are very formative. So we have to really decide what we want to teach them. Sexism really sets in, often without us realizing it. It happens because we shepherd girls – much more than boys – into a restricted and narrow world. We teach them to be neat, clean, quiet, well-behaved and high-achieving (in ballet or music or schoolwork). We create uptight, cute little conformity machines, and wonder why they often implode into anxiety, self-harm and binge-drinking by mid-secondary school.

In the UK, schools don't help this because politicians (not educators) have imposed testing and assessments and all kinds of irrelevant pressures on even the youngest kids in reception class, or kindergarten. And it's easy for children to get that feeling at home too – that you have to be the best. Which is crazy. Life is not a competition. And even if it was, children grow smarter, stronger, and have better sensory systems and a greater love of learning if they are allowed to play free until the age of seven. At least.

THE CURSE OF PERFECT

Writers such as Oliver James in the UK and JoAnn Deak in the US (see recommended books) have expressed serious concern about girls' growing perfectionism about their own performance – about being, essentially, too good. It begins in primary school, with schoolwork, appearance, behaviour and sporting achievement; as they enter their teens it can result in girls controlling the shape of their bodies through diet and exercise to unhealthy levels. It can end in total mental collapse.

New research has revealed something very startling – that the most anxious girls today are often those with educated and affluent parents. A concern that our girls perform well academically is turning into something that actually undermines their success, and makes them very unhappy young women.

We've long known that boys are often disadvantaged in early schooling because they don't like having to sit still, and are slower at achieving reading and writing skills because their brains develop more slowly. But it's likely that girls suffer an equally harmful consequence of formal learning too young. Because they are 'good' at school, girls may get lots of reinforcement – not for being themselves, or doing or making what they want – but for pleasing and conforming to what the teacher, or mum or dad, thinks is good. They develop what psychologists call an 'external locus of control' and think that their happiness depends on the approval of others. That's why it is so vital that we keep the under-six years free from formal learning, and allow children's natural capacity for self-directed play to develop, leading to strongly motivated, active and creative learners.

Your daughter needs, at this age, to feel FREE. That the world is hers to explore, that it is a rich and beautiful place and she can gain the competencies to navigate it safely. 'Free' doesn't mean free to be selfish or mistreat others, or to be heedless and stupid (or wander in the traffic). You'll sometimes have to sort her out on that. But it does mean trusting that intelligence grows, people skills develop, strength and confidence, even wisdom and inner peace, arise from being in direct contact with the living world through play. On the outside, and inside, in her own mind – you need to get your daughter exploding into an exploratory life. As feminism puts it, a girl's place is EVERYWHERE.

HOW NATURE BOOSTS HER INTELLIGENCE

A couple of years ago a strange thing happened. Two books came out with the same title, *Wild*.

One was a true story, which became a wonderful film, about a young American woman who had been very self-destructive, addicted to men and to drugs and full of insecurity. When the wonderfully named Cheryl Strayed's mother suddenly died, it triggered her descent into a free-falling lifestyle that seemed set to kill her. She finally decided to heal herself, not through therapy, but by walking thousands of miles along the Pacific Crest Trail. And it worked.

The other book was by a British woman, also a superb writer. Jay Griffith described how important it is to spend time in wild nature, let it fill your mind, and get away from the artificial and deadening environments of cities, buildings, electronics, deadlines and rush. Griffiths lived among indigenous people all over the world to research the book. She followed this book with another, called *Kith*, which argued that children need a home territory, a landscape, a place with both natural and human dimensions, which they are free to roam in during childhood. That having a home territory you are bonded to is the basis of wellbeing. In a world where we often move from city to city, and live in apartments far above city streets, this is quite a challenging idea.

It's hard to do justice to these books in a few words, but they won worldwide acclaim, in their own way, for depicting how womanhood could break out of its chains, and how *girlhood should never be chained in the first place.*

One of the most important things to know about your daughter is that she is a wild creature, and needs to stay that way to be healthy and reach anything like her full potential. By the age of one or two, she will be well ready to venture out into the world of nature, put bits of it into her mouth, climb, poke, chase small lizards, collect feathers and build twig houses, and get in touch with her inner elf. (That's not a misprint!) These are not just diversions or pleasant interludes from the real business of childhood – they are what childhood is for. Our eyes, ears, hands, limbs, feet and, ultimately, our brain need the complex and richly sensory world that only nature can provide. Rough ground makes our feet and limbs grow stronger, our brains more agile.

Please understand: the message isn't just 'it's healthy to get outdoors'. It's that in the complexity and richness of the natural environment, a child's senses begin to work at a significantly more refined and detailed level. (Just one example – 20:20 vision is simply the normal level – it's possible to have 20:10 vision. And there are comparable increases possible in smelling, hearing, touch, and sensorimotor awareness). When this begins to occur, then your daughter's brain also perceives more holistically, and sees the relatedness of the environment. A surprising number of the world's best thinkers and researchers were immersed in nature to an unusual degree, and their brains are different and better as a result.

BUSTING THE STEREOTYPES

The ideal of the neat, tidy, pretty, domesticated girl of times gone by still seems to be hanging on in our idea of girlhood. And in fact it's being made worse by the new fashion-and-frills dressing habits of our crazy consumerist time. If your clothes are cutesy pink and fluffy and cost a bomb, then you aren't going to be playing in the mud.

Personally I think the words 'kids' and 'fashion' should never be seen together. Kids should dress for warmth, mobility and the kind of individuality that they can create themselves without ever going near a shop. Dressing our kids up to be cute can be fun for adults, and a little won't kill you, but it's the razor's edge of turning a girl (or boy) towards self-consciousness and focusing on how they look, which in this era of massive anxiety about looks will be total poison to their mental health.

And then there are toys. We got rid of the little ovens, washing machines and toy irons that girls had in the 1950s, but substituted false eyelashes, pouty fishnet stocking dolls, pink pretty princess outfits ('some day my prince will come') and cut-to-the-crotch dancewear. Not exactly progress.

My sister actually had one of these, a toy iron! You could put a battery in it and it lit up the 'on' light. That's all it did! So she could have fun practising ironing. Just like mother!

It isn't a bad thing for kids – of both genders – to play at being grown up. Making food, building houses, playing at being families. But when toys are made that way – and there is a girls' aisle and a boys' aisle in the toy store – then we have a problem.

The real solution to sexist rubbish foisted on girls (along with not buying it) is to make her so strong and free, so early, that she just laughs at this stuff at eight, or fourteen. So the answer is – girls need wilding! You learn this through making messy artwork and building stuff in the backyard, gardening, and making things from mud and leaves. And mum and dad joining in. Through dancing and leaping about in the living room to loud music with mum and dad and friends. In having and keeping animals, fish and tadpoles, and growing every kind of plant. And whenever possible, being in the rain, woods, and on the beach. Encourage her to be messy, uninhibited, alive and moving about. Never complain about the state she gets in. Choose her clothes to be dirt-proof and damage-resistant, water-excluding or so sturdy it doesn't matter. And whenever you can, get outdoors into natural places and let her run free.

So here is a quick assessment on the natural wildness opportunities your daughter has (tick any that fit):

☐ **1.** My daughter is frightened of soil. She rarely ventures outdoors.

☐ **2.** We live in an apartment or flat where there is very little nature around.

☐ **3.** We have a garden or a park nearby, and do go there sometimes.

☐ **4.** We get out into nature whenever we can, have a pet, and do a lot of playing outdoors.

☐ **5.** We live in the countryside, and she plays in wild woods and I have to get twigs out of her hair.

And on inner wildness:

☐ **1.** Our family is neat. We are quiet. Our goal is achievement. That takes discipline and there is no room for messing about.

☐ **2.** We do occasionally let our hair down and it's actually quite good fun.

☐ **3.** Our daughter/s are very happy making a creative mess with paints and paper and glue and bits of stuff. They get it all over themselves, but it's nothing a warm bath won't fix.

☐ **4.** Our kid's favourite activity is wild dancing to loud music in the kitchen and living room. Everyone goes mad. When we go to mountain tops we end up shouting our names very loud.

If you ticked 1 or 2 on these two lists, don't panic!

That's what this chapter is to help you with. Please note – wildness should not be confused with being chaotic, disorganized or lacking routines. Kids and families do work best with boundaries and structure. You can only be truly wild when you know not to cut yourself, and there isn't cat poo on the bathroom floor – at least, not from last week. And especially if you don't own a cat!

EVERYONE CAN DO IT

Not everyone can live beside the woods, or the beach, or in a village where you can walk safely about with friends when you are seven. Where you can light a fire and make toast, or create your own shelter and wait with your dad to watch a badger emerge from its den at dusk. But can you see how wonderful and enlivening and freeing such a childhood could be? And begin to bring even some of that into your daughter's world? Even in the city, adventure is there. And nature can be found somehow, even just on holidays. So have that kind of holiday or weekend whenever you can. Many women remember being a child, totally blissed out on their first time on a lonely beach, or a hilltop they walked up with mum or dad, where they could see for miles around, and the wind blew in their hair.

> " Our daughter would play with sticks, pebbles, pieces of leaf and strange insects for hours in our garden. (And we lived in a place where there were snakes, large lizards called goannas up to a metre long, swooping kookaburras and sometimes hawks or eagles.) Her attention span was so great that it wasn't even a 'span' at all, it flowed all day long. She would make up stories, voice the dialogue between the characters, breaking off only occasionally to bring something to show us or to get something to eat or drink.
>
> *Jasmine, 37*

Can you see how, added together, these experiences might immunize her – even just a little – against the stupidities of social media or putting on make-up and fretting about being hot enough for boys?. From being cruel to friends. From needing to take drugs to feel good at fifteen.

And of course, the best wilding she can receive she learns from you, her mum and dad. If you demonstrate a free and exuberant nature, laugh, sing, dance, love nature, love music, love life, then she will just catch that as naturally as breathing. She will see a competent, caring, protective person, who is nonetheless unfettered, unconventional, untamed. Who takes joy in the moment and draws her out of reticence into exuberance.

THE VERY HELPFUL ROLE OF DADS

Dads have proven to be very valuable in helping girls be explorers. It's known from research that dads do more adventurous, active and physical kinds of play with girls than mothers do. They take children to wild outdoor settings and participate in riskier activities (and have more accidents, so do be sensible). Daughters with dads get knocked over by waves at the beach, graze their knees, wrestle, run and climb things far more. They go fishing. Dad is slightly less aware of mealtimes or having a balanced lunch! Within reason this can result in girls being more stress-resistant and hardy. But better still, they will be comfortable in male company, able to meet boys on their own terms. So dads – do stuff with your girls! (There's a whole chapter about this later in the book.)

Keeping Out the Hyenas

It's incredible how aware small children are of the world around them. So we have to be alert about the media that floods into our homes – television, the internet and magazines, as well as the advertising they see everywhere in the street, in shop windows and shopping malls. Advertising can accidentally impact our girls or be very deliberately targeted at them. In either case, its message is almost always harmful to their emotional wellbeing and self-image. We can choose what we let into our homes, and as they get older we can equip our girls to see what is being directed at them. We can fence out the hyenas until they learn how to fight them themselves.

> Selecting an outfit for the day ahead. Little Miss Two was at my side as usual, watching my every move. I chose my super-slimming high-rise black jeans, the ones that take a fair bit of jiggling to get on. It's about then that I notice my little blonde-haired girl waving her rear-end at the mirror. She's peering over her shoulder, gawking at her nappy-cushioned bottom, just like I do. The good old 'Does my bum look big in this?' move. I was shocked. I could've cried.
>
> *Claire, 39*

> When she was barely three, our daughter was playing on the carpet in front of the TV. We were in that half-daze of early evening, sitting chatting about something, when her voice rang out loud and clear. She had raised her head and was looking at the TV.
>
> 'Isn't that nice! That lady's husband will love her now she is thin.' My wife and I almost levitated in our rush to turn off the TV, while also looking casual and relaxed. The 'errkkk' feeling was so strong. Australian TV has ads – I am sure the UK does as well – for diet products that show vivid before and after footage of chubby people suddenly grown thin and happy. Our toddler had taken in every word.
> Love = thin.
> Woman = decoration.
> Marriage = goal in life. Aaaargghhh!
>
> *June, 33, and Daniel, 33*

About fifteen years ago the corporate world discovered girls. Marketers realized there was an untapped demographic that was the softest target in the world. Large corporations routinely hire child psychologists who advise them on better ways to exploit and, if need be, harm children. Yes, big tobacco, big alcohol, and today's equally conscience-challenged corporates all had psychologists to help them. And it all ramped up with science behind it. In Third World countries, they dress mid-teen kids in smart clothes and expensive-looking trainers, and these kids give out cigarettes to other kids for free. And they don't worry about low tar. Just last year, in Australia, a wine company released a fizzy red drink in plastic bottles with little hearts printed on the label. And 8 per cent alcohol. Luckily alcohol products aimed specifically at the young are now illegal, and this new product was quickly withdrawn. (But it took us almost twenty years to get those laws passed.)

By the early 2000s it really got serious. What these hired experts told the companies was that girls are different to boys in an important way. They are wired for social cueing. If two girls are friends in primary school and one of them frowns or scowls, the other one will worry about it all day. If two boys are friends, they will sometimes have a big fight – blood will flow – and in minutes it will be all over! Boys forget. Or more to the point, they barely notice in the first place. We have to teach our boys to be aware of other people's feelings. Most girls think about them all the time.

With this information, and some other insights I am not going to tell you, the advertisers focused millions of marketing dollars onto a new target – the pre-teen girl. In fact it was advertisers who invented the 'pre-teen girl'. As if being eleven is only about waiting to be a teenager, and not a

worthwhile age on its own. (Children are not pre-anything. They are who they are, and should be allowed to be so.)

Those advertisers succeeded beyond their wildest dreams. Forty per cent of ten-year-old girls now worry about their weight and actively modify their food intake in unsuccessful and harmful attempts to change their size and shape. It's sad because all girls get chubbier in the six months before puberty begins, and this is necessary for sufficient oestrogen to be built up. All old societies knew this and welcomed it. (Looks-conscious mothers and thoughtless fathers today say 'Whoa, you're getting fat!').

And so it goes. Girlhood has lost four precious, creative, confidence-boosting years. Ten-year-olds are fashion-conscious (or to put it more accurately, 'fashion anxious'). Twelve-year-olds are mortified to wear the wrong label, or not be seen with the cool soft drink or snack foods. Fourteen-year-olds spend their pocket money on make-up that their fresh young faces patently don't need. And one girl in twelve will develop an eating disorder as she struggles to fit an impossible body image she has seen thousands of times in magazines, her weight rising and falling like a yoyo with dieting that puts her metabolism into panic mode.

Sixteen-year-olds beg their parents to get them boob jobs or labiaplasties (yes, that means what you think it does). And on it goes.

There is only one way to avoid this, and it's to stop the media tsunami right at your door. Let's talk about that now. It begins with you.

I am in a large school auditorium, talking about *Raising Girls*. Midway through the evening I spring a surprise on my audience. I ask them to 'put your hand up if you are not happy with your own body'. And then we watch the result. You can do it here, right now (tick the one that comes closest):

1. ☐ I wish I could trade in my body. There are so many things about it I don't like.

2. ☐ I basically like myself the way I am. Maybe I would fix a few things.

3. ☐ I love my body unconditionally. It's a wonderful thing, and I feel tender towards it and grateful for its existence.

In my audiences, about 98 per cent of the hands go up. Only two in a hundred would tick option 3 above. But option 3 is where we need to be if we are to help our daughters escape this fate.

Here's a personal story from my own adolescence.

AN EXPERIMENT FOR YOU

Try this idea on for size – how would your life be if you decided right now that you loved your body as it is? How would that feel? If every time you saw or thought about your body, you cherished it and loved it? Might it lead to your being kinder to yourself, possibly even healthier? Can you see how that's not an if or a when (I lose weight, get my nose fixed) but it's a change of how you think. Just dropping the harsh, judgemental attitude you have to your own physical form, and appreciating it for the miracle it is. And how, if you were to make that change, it just might save your daughter's life?

One day, probably even before she is a teenager, most likely, your girl is going to come to you and say the following words. 'I hate my body.' Those are horrible words to hear. And you are going to want to say to her: 'You are beautiful! You look great!' But you won't have much credibility if she has seen you worrying about your weight, skin, hair, looks and clothing all her life.

> I am thin – really thin. I kind of like myself this way: my body is strong and does pretty much everything I ask it do to. I love my body because it's miraculous and has carried me through sixty years. But when I was a teenager I was very unhappy with how I looked. Our school was poor, and so when the summer came, we marched to the beach for our swimming lessons. In the changing rooms I would hide, and not come out, not take off a shred of clothing, until all my schoolmates had disappeared into the water. I would stay well away from everyone else in the waves (especially girls). I hated how my body was, and no amount of bullworkering or weight training made much difference. So what I am saying is – all teenagers go through this. We all want to look great.
>
> But today, that pressure is ten times worse. So we have to be sure we keep that pressure out of our homes. And that starts with you – their mum. Or dad.
>
> *Steve, 63*

Try this evaluation. Tick the ones that are true:

☐ **1.** Do you diet to lose weight, and talk about it?

☐ **2.** Do you have fashion magazines lying about your house, showing impossibly skinny women?

☐ **3.** Is shopping for clothes a major recreation for your family, or a bonding thing you do with your daughter?

☐ **4.** Do you ever speak critically about the weight or looks of other people in front of your daughter?

☐ **5.** Do you ever speak critically about your own appearance in front of her?

☐ **6.** Is putting on your make-up a big thing for you?

If you ticked more than two of the above – well, that's something to think about. Really think about. Because it suggests that looks are really important to you. Which might be harmless for you, but in today's world, it might be dangerous for your daughter.

Have a think about how you would like it to be for your girl. One day your daughter will be at school. Some boy, an idiot boy who probably actually likes her, will say to her in the playground 'You're fat!' She will turn to him, toss her head, and say 'I love my body. I bet I can make it to the fence quicker than you', and off they will run. Or he will

prove to be a total idiot, who doesn't deserve the second chance she just gave him. And she will never speak to him again.

What matters is that she is already so strong in her self-belief that she just sees him for what he is. Clueless and badly raised. But she will only be able to say this if one thing has happened. If she has heard you say those exact same words: 'I love my body.'

So, first you have to get your own act together. You abandon any looks obsession and start making your life about more important things.

Circle the below paragraph, if you agree with it. If not, this is an example your daughter can proudly follow.

'I think I need to stop putting so much importance on how I and those around me look. There are more important things in life. I want my daughter to love her body, so I have to love mine too.'

Well done! I would put the book down right here, and go out in the sunshine and sing. That's a huge breakthrough to acknowledge. Your therapist would give you a hug for that!

But if you are still here, well, I am too. Once we have our own house in order, then we are more than half way there. Then there is the next step – what the world teaches our daughters.

MANAGING MEDIA

There is a big decision that you have to make when you have kids, and you have to make it almost from the moment they open their eyes. That is, how much screen-based media you are going to have blitzing them in your home.

Tick the statement that best reflects your screen use:

☐ **1.** In our family we don't even own a television.

☐ **2.** In our family we limit screen-use to specific times.

☐ **3.** We have screens on most evenings all evening, and often in the mornings.

☐ **4.** Meals are eaten in front of a screen.

☐ **5.** Some sort of screen is always on in the house.

☐ **6.** A screen is always on in the house. My daughter also has a screen in her bedroom, this makes for less arguments and a more peaceful family life. I hardly see her apart from when she comes to the fridge.

It's just one person's opinion, but I would say if you are anything south of point 2, there's a problem. Here's why – screen use in your living room does several things that seriously change your family time. First of all, it really inhibits conversation. You won't talk for more than a few sentences because what's on the screen will grab your attention or, more importantly, your listener's. Nobody will bring up anything deep or important, because the atmosphere isn't right. The result is that, at least in that part of the house, couples don't communicate. Kids don't confide. Topics don't get discussed. News isn't shared.

There is another surprising, and alarming effect of this which has recently come to light. Studies are backing up what teachers have been noticing with alarm. Kids are coming to school who can barely speak. They can't make sentences. They just utter a few words here and there. They can't tell a story – even 'We went to the shops with Mum, I got a new toy train.' They can't hold a conversation. This is happening all over the world. The difficulty a lot of kids have in learning to read is now being reframed as an inability to actually string words together in the first place. Short utterances, that aren't grammatical, don't lead anywhere, and have no sequencing, are all that is left of the ability most five-year-olds once had to tell long stories and do so interestingly. And if a child can't do that, they can't think or reason either. This is down to one thing. At home, people are not talking to their children enough. And watching, even though it's all talk, isn't the same. It's not interactive. It doesn't involve them responding. So they don't learn.

Toddlers and small children don't even play properly if a show is playing in their earshot. In a quiet room, toddlers make up dialogue and have their dolls or action figures talk to each other in long and elaborate dramas. If a television or radio is playing for instance, though, they don't do this. Their attention span and their imagination both fail to develop.

And last of all, the big problem that everyone is focusing on – how media affects your daughter's

woman is a thing to be scrutinized. And a thing to be used.

Social media, selfies and eventually dating apps, hook-up apps and sexting just build on this. It can start to make a girl feel quite bad. A mum or dad who worries a lot about how they look. A culture that worries about how everyone looks. A snowstorm of never-ending depictions of people based on how they look. Is it any wonder we have this problem with girls?

SO WHAT TO DO?

There is plenty you can do:

1. **Never have television in kids' bedrooms.**

2. **Don't have mobile phones or iPads or computers in bedrooms if they are online, until at least the age of 16.**

3. **Only use television for watching specific shows, then turn it off.**

4. **Eat meals together round a table, and make it a happy, light kind of conversation when you do.**

5. **Don't make clothes shopping your main family recreation or way of bonding.**

6. **Encourage and support all the other things in life that are so much more fun than looking in the mirror.**

Just some ideas. To toss around.

self-image. Each day, with a programme playing in the living space, as well as from magazines, billboards, and online, your daughter sees thousands of thousands of images of women looking pretty, decorative, cute, groomed, sleek and thin. Is it any wonder that, consciously or unconsciously, she soon thinks that's what you have to be? She makes comparisons with how she looks, and slowly, gradually, feels despair. After quite a short time, the messaging of the ads mean that she sees herself as a product, and she sees products – the things you buy in shops – as being the key to being a better product herself. She decides that visuals – what your outside is, how others see you – matters more than how you feel, or act. That a

The
Chance
to be Wild
and Time
to be a Child

In a Nutshell

A big part of raising a happy girl is making sure she has a childhood, and it isn't cramped or curtailed by growing up too fast. That means two big things:

1. From the age of two, encouraging her to be a wild explorer, in the outdoors, in her mind, in creativity. Set her spirit free. Don't fence her in with ideas of being neat, girly, cute or compliant. Dress for action. Live free and wild.

2. Keep your house free of the insane media pressures about how you look. Make sure you yourself aren't hung up about looks. Don't have television on except for shows you specifically want to watch. Don't go clothes shopping or do looks-based activities with her until she is well into her teens. And maybe not even then.

From two to five is the time of play. A girl should emerge from this full of energy and confidence, and bursting to get into the larger world.

Chapter Three

Friendship Skills

" Friendship is important. It's also quite complex. It's the years from five to ten when the learning is at its most intense, but it continues right through life. In fact, most of us are still learning! "

The *Raising Girls* book began with Mollie, aged two, at playgroup. Mollie was about to smack a Tonka truck down on her little friend's head. Her mum saw this about to happen, and gave her 'the look' from across the room. It was a close call! It takes a fair bit of maturity to do friendship well, and the learning starts young. We parents do a lot of intervening and rescuing hurt feelings, over many years, before our daughters really get it right. This chapter will give you a great map of how to do this, especially if it wasn't easy for you in your girlhood. Perhaps it will help you too!

We human beings are social animals – we live, work, play, and learn in group environments. Even little babies make friends, and as we go through childhood, and then our adult lives, friends matter more and more. True friends are what make life bearable in the bad times, and so much happier in the good.

Girls naturally vary in temperament, and it's important we don't force sociability onto them. Some girls are most content on their own or with just a quiet friendship with one other person. Others are only happy in a buzzing, chattering group. Some are natural leaders, others prefer to follow. But even the shyest girl needs to learn enough 'people skills' to get along when she has to, and often the enjoyment of others grows when you learn how to make it work. You will be her natural coach in this. Often it's about finding a balance – if she is too bossy, or too compliant, too insensitive, or oversensitive, too trusting, or not able to trust, then she might need your help to find the middle ground.

While you are thinking about this, talk to your daughter! Ask her about her experience of making friends. Does she wish she had more, or different friends? Or is she having a lot of fun with her friends already? If she is struggling a little, or is young and just learning to be a friend, then make opportunities by visiting families with kids her age, having get-togethers with other mums, or help her join interest groups like Guides or activities based around her interests that are low in pressure and high in enjoyment.

So let's dive right in. Just off-the-cuff, how good is your daughter at being a friend? (Tick the ones that come closest.)

- [ ] **1.** A complete loner – she isn't really interested.

- [ ] **2.** She makes friends OK but it often ends in tears. She has a bit to learn, I think.

- [ ] **3.** Not too bad – a few bumpy times.

- [ ] **4.** Able to make and keep close friends.

- [ ] **5.** Able to get along with anyone and everyone.

IN THE YEARS FROM FIVE TO TEN

From the first day of reception or kindergarten, every parent hopes their daughter will meet and keep good friends and have things go smoothly. But in reality, there are always dramas! Friendship for girls causes enormous angst (a word that seems to have been created just for teenage girls!) But the good news is that these struggles are the way that they learn – as long as you are there to coach them when it all gets too hard.

In an excellent book called *Best Friends, Worst Enemies*, psychologist Michael Thompson describes seven key skills that make up friendship competence. I think it's a brilliant list. Here they are:

1. **A positive view of friendship (seeing it as valuable and fun).**
2. **Sharing and taking turns (essential with most games and activities).**
3. **Feeling for others (being unselfish and caring about the welfare of our friends).**
4. **Regulating aggression (not lashing out when we are angry, frustrated or sad).**
5. **Apologizing and meaning it (genuinely being willing to admit mistakes).**
6. **Reading emotions (understanding what others are going through from their looks and behaviour).**
7. **Trusting with caution (being able to trust, but having discernment, not being too gullible).**

Reading this list, you will see that many of the skills are a big ask – that is, they take a fair bit of maturity to master. But they really are the key foundations to being able to get along with others.

Let's use the list as our starting point to see where your daughter is at right now.

Give her a tick if she is good at the following skills, a question mark if not quite there, or leave blank if she doesn't have that skill yet.

☐ 1. She likes friends, values them and has fun with them.

☐ 2. She has learned how to share and take turns.

☐ 3. She cares about other children, not just herself.

☐ 4. She can hold back when she is angry, and doesn't hit or say mean things.

☐ 5. When she has done something wrong, she can say she is sorry, and actually is sorry.

☐ 6. She notices the feelings her friends are having and takes those into account.

☐ 7. She isn't gullible – she will trust others, but not unwisely (tick which is closest):

☐ TOO TRUSTING
☐ JUST ABOUT RIGHT
☐ TOO GUARDED AND UNWILLING TO TRUST

Looking at the statements you have ticked, you will be able to see which ones she is yet to master. Don't worry – even in girls as old as sixteen, there will still be gaps. But if you can pinpoint which ones are her vulnerabilities, you will be prepared when she comes to you seeking help.

I think my daughter most needs to learn about:

_____

_____

YOUR FIRST JOB –
BEING ON CALL

Your daughter's friendship 'issues' will mostly happen away from you, in her own world of school, sport, and so on. Places where you can't go, so you can't fix or control them, however much you might want to. Your role now is as a coach.

This means that you have to convey to your girl that you care and are available. You have to be the kind of person she can talk to. It's a tricky balance. One mother I knew was so anxious to be involved in her daughter's life that she quizzed her constantly, fretted over her and kept making interventions and suggestions to a maddening degree. Her daughter just became more and more private. The minute she was old enough, she volunteered for an aid project in the Amazon rainforest. That's a long way to go to get some personal space!

Usually, though, it's the opposite problem. Parents become so busy with their own stuff that they simply don't know what is happening in their children's lives. Or perhaps another, more needy sibling takes up all their attention. Whatever the reason, this can have terrible consequences. I was once called in to a school where a student had ended her own life. Her death was one of a spate of suicides in that city, which claimed some beautiful young lives and rocked the community. This fifteen-year-old had been horribly bullied, mostly online, by other girls at her school. She spent a lot of time online, and her parents, who had a lot of pressures of their own, had no idea this was going on. These tragedies are still thankfully rare, but kids bottling up stresses are not rare at all. Sometimes people simply misunderstand – they think teenagers are best left to themselves, that it's all about giving them more space. It's not. This is an age when, even

though they are separating and doing more on their own, they need to return to the 'mother ship' frequently and keep you up to speed with their lives and how they are going. So you have to be there. Not intrusive, but not hands-off either.

Here is a quick self-evaluation on finding the balance. Have a think about your own role with your daughter at the moment.

Put a tick next to which statement reflects your involvement:

☐ **1.** Overinvolved, intruding and crowding her.

☐ **2.** Somewhat overinvolved.

☐ **3.** Quietly present and available.

☐ **4.** I care but get a bit too busy.

☐ **5.** I haven't the time to know what happens in her world. That's her business.

Now for a little surprise – nobody ever ticks the first or last. Very few people would admit to those (or more accurately, those in those categories rarely see that they are). And so if you ticked No. 2, or 4, that means you might have to balance things up.

If you think you might be a bit overinvolved, then you have to begin giving her back the initiative. You just have to decide and be firm with yourself: 'She will tell me if there's a problem. I don't have to quiz her. My job is to be relaxed and available, so that she can talk to me in her own good time.'

It's important to remind yourself that your daughter's life is not yours. It can be as simple as, that having put so much into parenthood, you now find it really hard to step back. You may not have any other interests. It's important as your child becomes more independent to also find more independence yourself and branch out into activities that are just for you.

Therapists helping an overinvolved/overenmeshed parent often ask them to think about whether they are making up for something – their own loneliness perhaps. Or perhaps some guilt over something they haven't given her. Often if you are very anxious about your daughter, memories of your own childhood may be unconsciously contributing to this. Identifying these memories is often enough to let you release them and not put them on to her. A good clue to this is if you are having emotions, or reactions, which you sense are just too intense or out of proportion to what is happening. Of course, you may not know this, and it may take a friend, or your daughter herself to tell you. 'You're overreacting, Mum!' is a clue!

A counsellor can help if it's all just too tangled and you have lots of emotions that you know don't really match the here-and-now situation.

If you ticked the fourth option – 'a bit too busy' – well, it's not rocket science to figure out what to do about that! What activity would you be prepared to drop if you thought it would affect your daughter's mental health for life?

> I can't remember ever having a talk with my parents about my world, or my life. They yelled at me and my sisters to behave or stop fighting, or get the housework done. And then they busily rushed off. I can't remember ever in my childhood having my mum, or dad, sit down with me and ask 'How was your day? What is happening in your life?' Let alone have a talk. I didn't feel like a person in their eyes at all. They gave me a roof over my head. That was it.
>
> *Ali, 52*

She Will Test You Out

So, let's set the scene. It's late afternoon or early evening. Something has happened in your daughter's social world that day that has upset her. For some girls this can happen at least once a week.

If you have a close relationship, she will come to you for help. She will cruise by the kitchen or home office and check you out. If you look stressed, as if you don't have the 'bandwidth' to listen to her problems, then she won't bother you. Unless it's absolutely life and death, she will struggle on and worry on her own. While this is admirable, it is also the way that problems may start to accumulate.

Now – here's the thing. It's 99 per cent certain that you are pretty busy at this time of day. So it means that you have to master Parental Skill No. 17 – looking like you have all the time in the world. Then as you prepare the meal, sort the laundry, run your small business from a shelf on the landing, or wrangle a younger child out of their muddy clothes, she will come and talk to you.

And it will matter more than what you are doing. (Of course, if you know your daughter well, you can start to set aside time, or ask her to wait, or get in first when you are driving home from school.)

The very best way is that you and she have a time every day when you do catch up, so she knows that and saves her worries for then. But basically, if she comes for help, it's good to give her at least some of your time right there and then.

Being Unfazed

Here is something that it might be helpful to know. About 90 per cent of the time, her level of anxiety will be greater than it needs to be. That's because, from where she stands, it's huge, but from a distance of greater age and experience, it is simply part of learning about life. But you should never say this. What you do is stay calm, and ask her to tell you about it. The job of parents is to be less stressed than their children. (Most of the time; sometimes of course it's the complete opposite.)

The job of
parents
is to be less
stressed
than their
children

How It's Done

When our daughters come to us for help with friendship woes, it's important to slow things down. We first have to engage with them and show that we care. This means actively confirming what they are telling us. 'Wow, were you angry that she did that?' By double-checking the facts and the feelings, by giving a summary of what you have understood her to say, you are taking a journey with her into her world, getting alongside her and showing you understand.

Always spend a few minutes getting inside the problem and her feelings before you even attempt a remedy or solution. When she has calmed down a little, think about which of the seven friendship skills it might be that applies here.

Perhaps she is discovering that her best friend Zara is not good at skill 3, caring about others' feelings. She might be re-evaluating her as a friend. Perhaps your daughter needs a bit more of skill 7, not always being too trusting, learning that it's OK to be a little more wary – some kids just aren't all that constant. By learning to gauge character, she can see that the problem is not really her. For some girls, that's really important. Talk it over. Keep track of how it goes. Often kids' problems have evaporated in a day or two, as they are simply getting on with life, and don't need reminding of the bad times. By being a bit casual, you help her to be less intense. But do keep an eye open, especially for her general moods and how she is. There's always a reason when kids are out of sorts, and it helps to know what that might be.

Having this kind of structure to the conversation – listen, explore, analyse – she will start to sound more relaxed, calmed down, and ready to get on with her evening. You can check the next day how it all worked out, but be prepared for it to be ancient history now, or replaced by new and different developments!

YOYO FRIENDS

In an excellent (if rather obsessively detailed!) book, *Little Girls Can Be Mean*, by Michelle Anthony and Renya Lindert, some great insights are given about friendship in the under-eights.

One common hazard in your daughter's social world is the 'Yoyo friend'.

Yoyo friends are girls who warmly cultivate a friendship with your daughter, but suddenly change and are mean to her. Then, when she is really upset and confused, they start being nice again!

The authors imply that girls who do this are quite disturbed, and clearly their show of friendship is manipulative, rather than genuine. If your daughter encounters this, giving the benefit of the doubt for perhaps once round this merry-go-round seems OK. But if it happens again, your girl should probably back away from this person and make other friends instead.

It's generally good at this age to have multiple friends if possible. As a parent, you can help by having different/multiple girls to your house, so forming an open and welcoming friendship base, and by encouraging your daughter to be friendly to children who might be somewhat excluded too. Some quieter girls will of course just stick with a special friend, but if there is a willingness to at least play and have kindly exchanges with multiple children (boys and girls) then it lessens the ups and downs of depending on just one friendship. And sometimes kids just need a bit of a break from each other.

Anthony and Lindert believe that before the age of about eight, meanness is mostly unintentional, simply the effect of thoughtlessness and immaturity. Little kids don't always have the brain power to understand the effects of their actions. But from eight and onwards, meanness is more intentional. Kids know what they are doing. It is important to work with them to understand the impact of their actions on others, and the benefits to everyone of being kind, not leaving others out, not name-calling. There will always be kids from insecure backgrounds or not-very-loving families who are hurtful and controlling, but most kids learn to have empathy for others and treat each other as they would want to be treated. If you can help your daughter to make that leap (imagining herself in others' shoes) then she is well on the way to being a great human being.

reply, is enough. But if it's protracted or causing harm, then the school or teacher should intervene. Most schools now specifically teach bullying awareness in the classroom, teaching what to do, and committing their teachers and other staff to be a resource and respond actively. By getting it all out in the open and calling it what it is, a lot of bullying's power is taken away. It's the job of adults – especially in schools – to make sure discussions are held and really chronic bullies are given some serious attention. They are often quite disturbed or neglected kids – there is always a reason they are acting that way, and this has to be explored and the behaviour dealt with. It's not OK to do nothing. If nothing is being done, change schools. No child should have to endure meanness or intimidation every day of their lives.

BULLYING

Research shows that boys use more physical bullying – hitting, grabbing, pushing, damaging possessions, stealing lunch money and so on. Pretty horrible stuff, usually done in a group or to a smaller boy or girl. While some girls do this, most of the time they use 'relational bullying' – excluding a girl from the group, calling names, being sarcastic, spreading rumours. And, of course, the internet, texting and social media really lend themselves to this, amplifying it and making it a 24-hour thing if girls are allowed to have mobiles in their bedrooms. Relational bullying can do just as much harm and damage to health and happiness. It can lead the victim to self-harm, or even suicide in extreme cases.

Sometimes talking over with your daughter how to respond, whether to ignore, or how to

BULLYING AND YOU

Were you bullied as a child?

☐ **1.** Hardly ever

☐ **2.** Occasionally

☐ **3.** At one particular stage

☐ **4.** Often throughout my childhood

Was this by:

☐ **1.** Children at school?

☐ **2.** Siblings?

☐ **3.** Both?

When you think about this today, how do you feel?

☐ **1.** Does your heartbeat rise and do you feel anxious just remembering?

☐ **2.** Does your body have strong physical sensations such as your stomach churning or tensing, or your muscles tightening?

☐ **3.** I feel OK now, I have recovered from that.

Does your daughter's school deal effectively with bullying?

☐ Yes   ☐ Mostly   ☐ No

(For example, do they teach about bullying in the classroom, have clear guidelines for who to talk to and an ethos of speaking up for each other, and deal with cases properly to get help for both the victim and the children doing the bullying?)

It's natural and appropriate to feel both protective and angry when your child is bullied, and to have that spur you to take action. But be watchful of how much your own buttons are being pressed. You may easily find yourself becoming too emotional (and in danger of making matters worse). She needs you to be steady, calm and strong. Having a child bullied can be a trigger for some of us, and it's fine to get some counselling or at least talk to a friend and heal some of the distress from our own childhoods around this issue. Then you will be more able to help her effectively, and feel better in yourself for having done it in a good way.

TOO MUCH
TOO SOON

There is a bigger reason why things have become so mean and nasty in girl-land. It's about the values around us. If life is all a competition – to be the prettiest, hottest, most popular, or the smartest in tests, or most athletic, then it's a miserable world for our daughters. There is no chance to just be who you are, or relax and find your own unique path. And competitors can never really be friends.

Remind yourself, and her, often, that happy people aren't worried about competition – they enjoy doing what they like, being who they want to be, and making friends and having fun. In many schools there are subgroups of individualistic, nonconformist kids who are much more accepting and warm-hearted.

Same-aged peer groups (for such long periods of time) are not such a natural phenomenon, and so are often dysfunctional. We need more aunties, older kids, cross-age friendships, and more child-adult connection so that the peer group influence is less important. There is a rule in family therapy that a young person who is too influenced by the peer group is often the one who is not close to their same-sex parent. So a girl not close to her mum seeks nurturing and belonging from peers who are not well equipped to provide that. Of course, mid-late teens naturally move more into peer group belonging as part of growing up, but that's not true for five-to-fourteen-year-olds. Staying close to our daughters (mums and dads) means that they have safe harbours. Activities where people of different ages unite around interests and activities can be a wonderful broadener of her sense of uniqueness and worth. In Chapter 7 we will talk about this a lot more.

DOES MY DAUGHTER
HAVE ASPERGER'S?

Almost everyone now has heard of Asperger's Syndrome, which describes those who are on the autism spectrum but have fairly high intelligence and function well, except socially.

For a long time Asperger's, and autism generally, were less often diagnosed in girls. But now researchers think that this was mistaken. It's now thought that girls may be better at covering their social difficulties, but have to work so hard at this that they often suffer from acute anxiety or depression. 'Aspergirls' are often mistakenly diagnosed with anxiety disorders or obsessive-compulsive disorder, when these are actually a response to the difficulties they have in understanding social situations. So it's important to know what girl-version autism spectrum disorders look like, and give these girls the right care and support.

While a professional diagnosis is always recommended, some of the most obvious signs will be things you may be very familiar with. Have a look at the list on page 81, but also be aware that autism is very diverse. Not all girls on the spectrum are the same. It's probably not even correct to think of it as a spectrum – more of a tree. And in girls the boy-traits often portrayed in the media are not as obvious – girls are better at finding ways to cope.

Nobody knew me. They only knew the pretend me.

People with Asperger's are often the inventors,
the innovators, and the ones who say
'we need a kinder, better world'.

1. She may have an unusual way of making eye contact. Rather than avoiding it as boys often do, she will have figured out that it matters and so keep eye contact for longer than most people do.

2. She will probably be articulate and have a great vocabulary, but speak in a slightly formal way – like an actor or a BBC announcer. It will be impressive, but just a bit unusual given the way most girls talk these days.

3. She may know a lot about a specific subject or interest area, and be very happy to share this with you. However, she doesn't manage the conversation very well, i.e. may speak for too long without giving you the chance to reply. This may be more noticeable when she is with new people and feeling anxious. You may feel concerned that she seems to be working too hard at the conversation. And this is usually correct.

4. Physically she may be somewhat clumsy or uncoordinated, even to the point of having an awkward way of walking. But not all girls on the spectrum have this trait.

5. Finally, and a very positive trait – she will likely be extremely caring for others and compassionate and generous, and this might extend to a strong commitment to justice, animal welfare, and proper treatment of children. She will be a loyal and generous friend – or daughter. There is a lot to like about girls with Asperger's.

The inner experience of having the condition, though, is very hard. She will notice at a young age that other people seem to socialize easily and enjoyably, but find how to do this baffling and have many misfires in the playground and with friends. She may work very hard to try and solve this – watching girls who are good at humour, friendship, leadership and so on, and very accurately mimic their sentences or expression or posture. But the sheer effort, together with a sensory overload which people on the autistic spectrum often have, through not knowing what to filter out – will lead to acute anxiety in many social situations, especially informal or unstructured ones – parties, playground groupings, small talk and so on.

It's a huge help if you know what's going on, and explain situations to her and what is expected, but also allow her to stay in her comfort zone. If your aspergirl doesn't want to stay in conversation with guests at the table, or be the life and soul of the party, let her know it's fine to chill out, not say much, and even excuse herself and have some quiet time to herself when she needs to. She may not know that it's fine to answer questions with just a couple of words, smile, and then just nod and listen. Knowing this can take a lot of anxiety from her shoulders.

Knowing they have the condition, and getting good support, help with deep relaxation to counter the stress, counselling with someone who has the condition or is very experienced with it, all help a lot. Outcomes, once diagnosed, are good – those with the condition continue to learn throughout their lives, and help can be more tailored, since the usual therapies which work with neurotypical people do not quite hit the mark.

Also, the onus is really on the larger world to appreciate and get comfortable with the fact that some of us are different. People with Asperger's are often the inventors, the innovators, and the ones who say 'we need a kinder, better world'. Treasure your aspergirl – she has so much to give and gain.

Friendship
Skills

In a Nutshell

Friendship is quite complicated, and the primary school years are the peak of learning how to make it work.

The skills of friendship include valuing friends, sharing, caring about others, managing anger, apologizing, empathy, and learning when and when not to trust others.

We need to be coaches for our girls when they bring home 'friendship angst'. This mainly means just listening, but sometimes we can make suggestions and help them understand which of the seven skills of friendship apply.

Bullying in girls is usually not physical, but relational bullying can be even more harmful. If it persists it may need skilled intervention by the school.

Chapter Four

The **Love** and **Respect** of a **Dad**

> " A father who is able to show his caring makes a huge difference to a girl. It's a learning curve, since her world is very different to yours. There are some secrets that make it a lot easier. "

Here it is in a nutshell: dads and father figures really matter to girls. Having two parents who love you – and show it – is an amazing feeling. But there is more, because dads are different. Dads are big, hairy, often quite exciting and lively, and interested in different things to mum. And because he is the first male presence in her life, a dad is an example of what to expect from the whole male gender (so, no pressure!). Also, every girl has a masculine side to her as well, which she incorporates her dad into. She takes qualities from dad and mum and mixes them into the kind of person she wants to grow into.

For at least 90 per cent of girls, males will be the gender they are most interested in as a potential partner, and so she will see you as a template. If you are kind, interested, respectful to her mum, not loud or scary, have time for her and love to do things with her, then that will set the benchmark for all her relationships with boys and men. She will expect nothing less, and settle for nothing less. The research shows that a caring dad is a strong protective factor for girls in preventing bad things happening, and correlates with improved school results, career success, self-esteem, and staying away from alcohol or drug misuse. That's a pretty impressive list.

Fathers today are very different to those of the past. Dads in the past were often rather distant, or busy, or were scary and yelled a lot, and so many girls didn't get good fathering. Today that's really turning around. This chapter will help you be the kind of dad that daughters love, and draw on for their whole lifetime as a source of life and strength.

> I thought I was a good dad because I worked really hard to support the family. I thought that was all a dad had to do. My daughters made me realize that just wasn't true. It's your time that they want the most.
>
> *Noel, 47*

> You have to loosen up, especially if you have this great plan for how things are going to go. Things never go that way! We had this canoeing activity all figured out. But our two-year-old just wouldn't be in it! After all that trouble. The old me would have kicked up such a stink – you ungrateful kid, you don't deserve these great things I provide, rah rah rah. The new, more experienced me, well, I just consider it from her point of view – maybe she was just scared. Maybe it wasn't such a great idea after all. So we mucked about on the beach, and she loved that.
>
> *Folarin, 35*

> You learn to let go. That's the key to happiness a lot of the time. You give them a toy, they play with the box. That kind of thing!
>
> *Edward, 52*

YOU AND YOUR DAD

Here's a story. I am leading a seminar with a group of parents in London. They've come from all over the country for an intensive day on raising daughters. In the afternoon, we watch a short DVD about fatherhood, which includes interviews with girls about their dads.

Two girls in their late teens – sisters – are talking about their father. The first one says 'I am an action girl! I love to do physical activity, sport, dancing, the outdoors. Dad was always available to do this with me. He always came along, was interested. Even stuff he just couldn't relate to, like dancing, he still sat through because he knew it mattered to me.'

Her sister now speaks. 'I am totally different. To me the thing that mattered most, growing up, was affection. I needed lots of reassurance. I knew I could get Dad's time pretty much every day, when I needed it. I loved to sit on his knee when I was young, and he never hurried me or sent me away. He never made me feel I was a nuisance.'

When the DVD ended and the lights came up, I noticed a striking thing in the room. The women, almost all of them, were completely silent. As I looked at the faces more closely, there were tears in many eyes. I asked – what's happening? There was a rush of comment. The women in the room had undergone two completely different reactions. Half of them were in tears because they had been reminded of their own dads, and how special and close they had been. *They were remembering how much they loved their dads*.

But the other half were in a different place. They were very sad, because their dads had just not come through for them. Hearing these young women speak on the film, they were intensely aware of *what they had wanted, but not received*. They so yearned to have been loved by their dads in this way.

A great benefit of this discussion was that the men in the room were incredibly struck by how much a father's attitude and behaviour had impacted on their partners and the other women – all these years later. It made many men, that day, decide to get closer to their girls.

IF YOU ARE A DAD

What kind of example of fatherhood was your dad, when you were growing up? (You can tick more than one.)

1. My dad wasn't around. I didn't really know him.

2. My dad was distant and remote. He kept his emotions to himself and didn't really show much affection.

3. My dad was explosive and angry, judging and criticizing those around him.

4. My dad was kind of a nothing, lost in his own problems. He got pushed around by my mother and I hated seeing that.

5. My dad was caring, but a little awkward. I do think he loved me though.

6. My dad was a fun guy, but didn't really have a strong side. You couldn't really count on him.

7. My dad was warm and affectionate, but also let us know when we went too far or did the wrong thing. He was warm, but had clear boundaries.

8. I always felt safe, and loved, around my dad. I would like to be as good a dad as he was.

Just thinking about this often brings many feelings and memories. If you had a great dad, that really helps. If not, *it's important to know you can be different to the dad who raised you.*

So this leads naturally to the next question. If you want to be different to your own father in any way, what would that be? (Tick the three most important differences.)

☐	safer	☐	more reliable
☐	kinder	☐	more sane
☐	stronger	☐	not abusing alcohol or drugs
☐	happier	☐	staying the distance, not running away
☐	more involved	☐	respecting his children
☐	more interested	☐	just less of a bastard all round!

or in your own words

_____

The first step is deciding how you want to be as a father. The second is to find out *how that is done*. We humans do most of our learning from 'role models' that we watch and copy. Our brains are actually very good at that. In making the change you want, one of the best things to help is to think of someone who has the qualities you would like to have. *Who do you know that is the kind of man that you would like to have had as a father?*

Of your friends and acquaintances, who is the best dad that you know?

_____

Nobody is perfect, and often men we know have both strengths and weaknesses. Sometimes what we need is a combination of different men, the playfulness of one, the strength of another, the 'open heartedness' of someone else. We guys put together our manhood by bundling parts of many other men we have known. It is a method that works very well.

We dads can adopt the qualities of different men we have known – the playfulness of one, the strength of another, the open-heartedness of someone else.

IF YOU ARE A MUM

Here is a self-evaluation for you as a mum of your experience of fathering. Many women have powerful positive or negative experiences of their fathers. It is such an important relationship, and in past decades was often very fraught.

(Tick the one that comes closest.)

☐   **1.**   The worst case scenario. I don't think my dad loved me. I think I was just a nuisance in his life.

☐   **2.**   I was never sure if my father loved me or not. Perhaps he did, but he didn't really know how to show it.

☐   **3.**   My dad was pretty good, I know he loved me deep down, but he was often just too busy. So we didn't really get or stay close.

☐   **4.**   My dad loved me fiercely, and he let me know that, with his actions and his words. I carry that love in every cell of my body. He was a wonderful dad.

Please – if this exercise is hard for you, let us send some love and warmth to you. You have somehow made it to parenthood and are caring a lot for your own children. *We want you to know you are very important and worthwhile – and always were.* And we hope you get to experience masculine caring of a more adequate, better kind, if you didn't get that. We men are slowly learning how to be more loving. I hope you encounter that.

For women, one of the consequences of having a not very good dad is that you may devalue the importance or potential of dads. Have a think for a minute if that might be so?

Do you think that you...
(tick the one that comes closest):

☐ **1.** Deep down decided that dads are not much use, and you didn't need one.

☐ **2.** Married a man, but didn't expect him to be an active dad, and maybe even found it hard to share the parenting with him.

☐ **3.** Set out to find someone who would be different to the father you had and be loving and kind.

☐ **4.** Had a great dad, and chose someone with those same qualities.

If you ticked 1 or 2, are you starting
to rethink that early decision?

☐ **1.** Yes, I am interested in how my partner could be more important to our daughter's life and want to encourage that.

☐ **2.** Nope. All men are bastards!

DANGERS FOR DADS

There are a number of common pitfalls for dads. The first is the scariness of puberty. Some dads get very awkward when girls reach puberty and start to withdraw their affection, for fear that it will be misunderstood as sexual. This concern is well-motivated, but be careful not to overreact. Many girls in the past felt a sudden coldness in their fathers when they reached puberty and began turning into a young woman. They felt that they had done something wrong, that he didn't like them any more. This was a sad and hurtful thing for them. Daughters still want to feel you care about them at every age. Your daughter may want more privacy, and not seek affection as much, but don't pull back if she seeks your warmth – she is the same girl and still needs to know you love her.

The second pitfall is what I call the 'provider tragedy'. Often we dads show our love by working hard at our jobs, but we are out of sight when we do this. We show our caring by going away and earning money. They just think that we don't care because we are busy, or tired. So our love doesn't come through. Often a girl would much prefer to have less gifts or money, but more of you being interested in talking to and doing things with her. She may feel more love from walking the dog with you, throwing a netball or going out for a hot chocolate, than any money you provide.

Because dads are the opposite sex, our comments and actions have a huge impact. Don't ever make negative comments on your daughter's appearance – weight, hair, shape, skin or the like. If you do, you may as well sell your house to pay the psychiatrist bills.

Ian, 46

I never ever got angry with my daughter, and had it work out well. Perhaps some girls need confronting sometimes, but I think it has to be still quietly and unthreateningly put across. Anger at daughters always just seems to make matters worse, and I have to backtrack and go into damage control.

Mitch, 51

Girls have more acute hearing than boys. Partly because of this, they hate shouting. It scares them and makes them feel unsafe. Talk gently to girls, and things will always go better.

Peter, 39

DR BRUCE ROBINSON

Dr Bruce Robinson AM is a Professor of Medicine at the University of Western Australia (UWA) and the founder of the National Centre for Asbestos Related Diseases. It was his work with dads dying from lung cancer that moved him to help make fatherhood more engaged and loving, and reduce the terrible distance that many fathers had from their children. He founded the Fathering Project at UWA, and is the author of three books, *Daughters and their Dads*, *Fathering from the Fast Lane* and *The Blue Book of Tips for Fathers and Father-Figures*. You can read more and find many resources for helping dads at **www.thefatheringproject.org**

TEN STRATEGIES FOR BEING A GREAT DAD (with Professor Bruce Robinson)

Now for something special. I'm going to let you in on the wisdom of one of the dads I most admire in the world (though it would embarrass him to hear that). We've been friends for longer than I can remember. Bruce Robinson is a Professor of Medicine, a chest surgeon, who after hearing so many lung cancer patients express such regrets about their lives, decided to improve things between fathers and kids. He created the Fathering Project at the University of Western Australia, and has reached tens of thousands of dads in a life-changing way. Here are his ten strategies – practical, simple and clear. They can change your life, and your daughter's. They certainly did mine. Here goes:

1. Dad Dates

In Bruce's experience, one of the simplest and yet most powerful strategies for fathers to connect to their children is to go out on regular 'dad dates'. If a dad bothers to spend time with each child, one-on-one, it generates an enormous feeling of worth. Bruce says the key to success with this is the 'NOANOK rule' – No Other Adults, No Other Kids. Just dad and one child at a time. He and his wife have both done this since their kids were quite young – dad dates and mum dates. Usually it's been dinner somewhere the kids choose (but not a fast food chain) and a movie or something similar.

And a cautionary note – Bruce told me he learnt very quickly that if you think dad dates are an opportunity to 'sort the kids out' you are wrong. If you do that, the kids will always avoid these dates.

They only work if dads listen and ask them about their friends and what they are enjoying or finding hard at school. If it becomes an inquisition or criticism it won't work. Make it light and friendly. Only go deep emotionally if your child takes it there.

2. Dad Trips

In one of his books Bruce wrote a chapter about how dads can take their kids on trips, including work trips. These again are one-on-one events. Some years later he was at a conference and the president of the society ran up and nearly hugged him as he recounted how he had read that chapter and his relationship with his teenage daughter had been transformed.

They were arguing and fighting all the time. He was desperate. So he took the opportunity to invite her with him on a conference trip to Paris. The conference lasted five days and they had another week and a half together as father and daughter.

He said that since they returned she had talked about nothing else but that trip and the special times that they had together. He even heard her telling people that it was the 'best two weeks of her life'. Then he stopped speaking, looked a bit teary, and said, 'You know what, Bruce? They were the best two weeks of my life as well.'

There is a magic about these trips. Again they follow the law of NOANOK. It doesn't have to be Paris, but it does have to involve some effort. Travel together, be away together and be intentional about spending this time to connect. How could a child or young person not conclude from this that you care about them?

3. Be Creative about Making Time with Kids

It's amazing how often men use work as an excuse for not spending time with their children. It is possible to be creative about making time. Bruce underwent a transformation himself with his daily routine. After surviving a life-threatening accident, he decided to begin walking to school with his kids in the morning. Like a lot of these things, he did it because he felt he 'should' but then ended up loving it.

There are other ways to work around the school day. Some men finish work early one day a week and take their kids to the beach or for an ice cream. It is also important to come home and have dinner with the kids and turn the television off during that time. Bruce discovered research that families who eat together four nights a week or more reduce the risk of substance abuse in their children by half. He has noticed how many kids moan to their parents about having to turn the television off and sit around the family table and then, twenty years later, say it was the best thing that ever happened.

4. Help Her Understand that She Is Special

Bruce once interviewed David Gower, the former captain of the English cricket team, about fathering. When he asked him what he thought his girls needed from him, to his surprise David answered, 'They need me to help them realize how special each of them is'. This is crucially important for any daughter.

Every child is special and once they realize this, all sorts of things happen. They don't need to put other kids down (they are free to appreciate how special other kids are). Also, they are less likely to take drugs as they get older – they have worth without them.

To help kids understand their specialness you need to understand what it is about each of your children that is unique. It may be their personality, their talents, the way that they show kindness, interesting things that they have done, pathways they have chosen to take, or many other things. It is much more effective to identify those specific things and encourage the child in them than to use empty phrases such as 'you are awesome' – kids spot that sort of hollowness very quickly.

And another important tip – help each of your children realize that they have a special future. They will probably never be famous, they don't need to be in the top team or get into medical school, but they have a unique and wonderful future that will be a gift to the world and you are looking forward to seeing it. They are here to live their own lives and not to live the life that you, as their parent, want them to live.

Another way to help them feel special is to seek and value their opinions. Ask them what they think about politics, holiday choices, football tipping or topics on the evening news. Importantly, avoid comparing any of your children to any other children inside the family or outside.

5. Practise Listening

When Bruce asks audiences of dads how good they are at listening, 98 per cent do not put their hands up – they know how bad they are at listening. It is hard for us dads to resist the urge to jump in and solve the problems our kids have, to tell them what they should do or to criticize them. Often that comes out of a feeling of love for them – we are afraid that they will do the wrong thing so we want to fix it. But this approach almost never works.

As a result, kids – especially teenagers – stop telling their dads stuff because they are afraid of the lecture that they are about to get. Bruce says he feels he is not a good natural listener himself, but 'I have learnt to superglue my lips together and listen to what they have to say.'

He suggests two useful strategies. First, avoid being the plumber or the policeman. The plumber fixes things – you don't need to do that. The policeman makes judgements and arrests – avoid being judgemental and critical.

Second, remember the word 'boomerang'. Most people in conversation boomerang the conversation back to themselves.

So when a teenager says something about being at a party and the difficulties they have resisting the peer pressure to smoke, drink or to take drugs, it is easy to boomerang back to yourself and say 'I remember when I was your age…' It is important to discuss your experience at some stage, but vastly more effective to continue to stick with what the child wants to say. Don't let your own feelings get in the way – when they talk about drugs it is easy to get panicky and overreact, but it doesn't really help.

6. Get Mobilized into the Values War

Our kids are subjected to an enormous amount of pressure from television, movies, magazines and peers to adopt a series of values that are different from ours. This pressure can be tremendously strong. Fathers are very powerful in establishing values in children, including values on sexuality, but if we don't discuss and model a different set of values we leave the kids vulnerable to those pressures.

Be specific with them about values like trust, honesty, integrity, showing respect to others and generosity to the poor. The best way is to model those values yourself in your attitude to your neighbours, immigrants and people who are disabled, obese or 'uncool'. They will be watching you and will learn about how they will deal with other kids at school – it will influence whether they become bullies or not.

Bruce is amazed at how many fathers have not talked to their sons and daughters about sexuality. Of course the kids are embarrassed, and they say they know it all already, but wouldn't you be embarrassed if you knew that your father was going to talk to you about sex?

He recommends a little trick that works well. Say to the kids, 'I know you know it all already, but I read in a fathering book that I need to do this and I'll feel really bad if I don't, so can you please humour me on this?' It works a treat. (Go to Chapter 7 to find out more about what to actually say!) It's not just about the plumbing. With teens there are other things to consider. The importance of consent. Of going slow, knowing the person well enough to be able to trust them. Of not hurting people. Of being safe about disease and pregnancy. Of only having sex when you feel totally right about it, and not when drunk or because of pressure to please someone else. Your kids may not always take this advice, but they will have to think about it.

7. Don't Assume that Your Kids Aren't at Risk of Drug Addiction

Every parent is frightened of their kids falling victim to substance abuse. Drugs are easily available in the community and are pushed very hard by individuals who are often addicts themselves and thus need the money. If you don't get involved in helping your kids resist drugs you are giving these pushers a 'free hit'.

Be aware of what drugs are around and identify the risks each of them poses to your kids. Find out from your kids what social and personal rewards they or their friends receive when they take drugs: i.e., acknowledge that there are reasons why people take drugs. Talk to them about peer pressure. When you talk to them make sure you also listen to what they have to say.

It's even more helpful if you can welcome their friends over to your house and get to know them – often those friends will be quite lonely and desperate for a father figure in their lives. One helpful trick is to teach children handy phrases to use when drugs are being pushed at parties. Tell them that being confrontational with comments like 'drugs are bad for you' doesn't help. What is more helpful is being able to 'pass'. Sorry, I have to play football/netball tomorrow' or 'sorry, I have to work tomorrow' works much better.

Bruce returns again and again to the principle that if you establish a good relationship with your child from a young age the chances of them becoming a long-term drug addict plummet. I should emphasize that a good relationship involves listening, fun times, helping kids feel special, as described above, and not being too critical or over-disciplinary. Research suggests that the most common factor related to substance abuse is not the absence of a father but the presence of an overcritical, over-disciplinarian father who makes a child feel worthless rather than worthwhile.

If you do discover that your child has taken drugs, don't blow a fuse. The Fathering

**NOANOK
rule.
No Other Adults,
No Other Kids.
Just dad and
one child
at a time.**

Project promotes a phrase for fathers to use when disciplining children which has been very effective. Instead of unloading your own emotion on them, a phrase such as 'I am disappointed, but I do believe in you and I know that you are better than that, and we will work through this together' is way more powerful. It strengthens rather than diminishes the child's sense of self and improves their likelihood of getting through that difficult time.

8. Be Involved in Her Education

Both boys and girls need to know that you value their education. Sit with your kids sometimes (or if they want, more often) while they do their homework and help them work through it. Begin to stimulate their curiosity from a young age by taking them on visits to places like museums and public libraries. One good idea when you take your kids to the museum or any other exhibition is to get them to look at everything and then come back and get them to tell you what their favourite two exhibits were.

Another good trick of Bruce's is called 'FART' time – this stands for Family Altogether Reading Time. It is when the whole family sits down, turns the television off and reads together. The word is a bit naughty so the kids love the idea of it.

Critical to kids' attitude to education is your attitude to the school and the teachers. Early on, Bruce used to complain about his kids' teachers, but he realized that it would be much more helpful if he could thank them for teaching his children and ask them how he could help. Dads who get involved at school build a bridge and make it easier for their kids to like and enjoy school.

9. Understand that Daughters Are Not the Same as Sons

The Fathering Project asked more than three thousand dads what their daughters need from them as dads, as distinct from their sons, and found that less than 1 per cent could answer this. Given the powerful effect of a father in a daughter's life, this is frightening.

Bruce is clear that dads need to be able to tell their girls regularly how beautiful they are, inside and out (not 'pretty', but beautiful inside and out). Daughters get signals from their dads about how they can expect to be treated by men. If dad treats her with respect then her bar of respect will be set high and she won't put up with crap from men – if he doesn't, then she is vulnerable.

Fathers have a profound effect on the likelihood that a girl will grow up and have a successful long-term relationship with a man. Indeed, the No.1 factor that determines the level of confidence a woman carries into her adult life is the relationship that woman had with her father. That he loved spending time with her, listened to her and talked softly and respectfully around her and around her mum.

10. Girls Are Vulnerable to Words

Girls have their radar out for what their father or another strong father figure thinks of them and it is vital not to overlook that. Whereas boys learn as apprentices to their fathers in shoulder-to-shoulder activities, girls are listening. How do you speak to her? How do you speak to her mum?

If your dad wasn't much good, choose to break the cycle. Many men have not had good role models. So it is tempting for dads to give up and leave the parenting to mum and just become a provider and protector. That does not work. You have to choose to break that cycle and become a good dad yourself.

Bruce's hero in this regard is Tony Cooke. Tony, a West Australian man, who you have probably never heard of, grew up in very difficult circumstances. His father Eric was a serial murderer and the last person to be hanged in Western Australia. This made things very difficult for Tony at home and at school. What is deeply impressive about Tony is that he is a wonderful man and a wonderful father. And he is very clear about the fact that he chose to break the cycle and learn how to be different.

It is unlikely that anybody reading this would have a background as bad as Tony's, so there is no excuse for not choosing to break the cycle. This involves being willing to learn about fathering (from books, seminars, fathers' groups) and then gradually putting into practice each of the things that other dads have found to be effective in particular situations.

That's a heck of a list. Don't worry, you can go back to it at other times for new ideas. But for now, if you are interested in setting some goals, then here is the list in simple form.

Tick the ones you already do.

☐   **1.** Having regular dad dates with just her.

☐   **2.** Having dad trips where dad and daughter travel together.

☐   **3.** Finding creative ways to make time together despite a busy schedule.

☐   **4.** Helping her know she is special in specific ways and has a unique part to play in the world.

☐   **5.** Listening to her without leaping in with advice, and valuing her opinions.

☐   **6.** Talking to her about values in how you treat people – trust, honesty, racism and sexism, respect – and how people treat her.

☐   **7.** Talking to her practically about drug use, peer pressure, what drugs are around and the risks. If she does use drugs, keeping the communication channels open around that.

☐   **8.** Being involved in her schooling.

☐   **9.** Treating her with respect, so that she learns she deserves that.

☐   **10.** Talking to her positively and gently, and also praising her in front of others.

That's great – well done! Then go back and choose two of the remaining ones, which you think you could possibly do, and which might work well with your daughter. Put a circle around those two. Don't overreach, just start to experiment a little with giving this a go.

A final note

These are new behaviours. We guys don't like to fail. Or even get out of our comfort zone. We have learned to fear vulnerability. But vulnerability is what love is all about. By trying to get it right with your daughter, you will melt her heart and heal any wounds you might have inadvertently caused in the past. A good man isn't someone who has it all together. It's a man who is willing to learn.

Warmest wishes to you as a dad. You are so important to your girl, and even just trying is the thing that matters.

The love you get back from a daughter for even trying to be a good father is one of the best things in life. For her life to go better because of you, it's so worth it.

The
Love
and
Respect
of a
Dad

In a Nutshell

 Fathers make a huge difference to girls.

In the past, fathering went through a bad time – not all of us had great dads.

We can learn to be much better than our own dad was.

There are ten practical things that dads can do. Choose one, and put it into action. See how it goes.

The best man is one who keeps learning, and is willing to be vulnerable trying new things.

Chapter Five

Spark

> " Every child has inside them an interest, ability or passion that is waiting to be discovered. That can become a focus of all their enthusiasm. That makes them want to be alive. How do we find what it is? How do we fan it into a bright fire? Why does it matter? "

Is your daughter over eight years old? If she is, then she's probably getting very engaged with the world outside the home. At school, but hopefully in other ways too. But how positive is that involvement? How much fun? How much does it grab her spirit and draw her along on the journey towards being a woman? This chapter is about finding the inner interests that will link her to the larger world.

Some girls wake up anxious every day. They check their phone for messages. They worry about a new pimple that is threatening their otherwise spotless face. They wonder how much breakfast they can eat without gaining weight. They are edgy and listless all day – school is boring, they have no sense of direction. We watch them and know in our hearts that this isn't right. Is your daughter like this? Do you ever sigh in exasperation at the gloom and unhappiness that seems to hover over our girls?

There are young people who are not like this at all. They are energized, interested in life and seem to have skipped the whole adolescent angst thing, or at least got through it in minimum time. What makes these kids different from the unhappy hordes?

The secret of a happy late childhood and adolescence may turn out to be something that specialists in adolescence have come to call 'Spark'. Spark is a metaphor – and a very good one – for the deep interests and passions that lie inside your daughter. Every girl has a spark or several (several is better). Our job is to help her find it, do the practical things to make it possible and then stand back and enjoy the ride. If you do, you will have a happier, more positive and much more fearless girl. Sounds like something you'd want?

Spark was first described by researcher Dr Peter Benson at the Search Institute in Minnesota. Benson was already world famous – his work on strengths in young people was a cornerstone of what became Positive Psychology and he has been cited in thousands of research studies since. But his Spark concept is the single idea that is changing most lives today. (You can google Peter Benson Spark and see his TED talk, which sets out beautifully how this all works. Or you can just read on!)

Benson's research team found that sports and arts (dance, drama, music, books, artwork, craft) are the most common sparks for young people. Animals – dogs or horses or animal welfare itself – are the third biggest. But it could be anything – rock hunting, orienteering or dressing up in medieval clothes and hacking each other with blunt swords!

START WITH YOURSELF

You can understand spark if you think of your own childhood. When you were a child, did you have an interest, hobby or activity that you loved? Have a go at this self-evaluation:

What was your spark as a child?

_____

_____

Did it change over time?

_____

_____

How much did your parents encourage it? (Tick the statements that fit.)

☐ **1.** Not at all.

☐ **2.** A bit.

☐ **3.** They encouraged but didn't do much to help.

☐ **4.** They encouraged, helped, paid for and enjoyed hearing about it.

Did this interest get acknowledged outside the family?

☐ YES   ☐ A BIT   ☐ NO

Did any adults at school know about your interest, or encourage it there?

☐ YES   ☐ MAYBE   ☐ NO

And lastly – what happened to your spark? (Tick one statement or more.)

☐   **1.**   It didn't last very long. Life just got too busy.

☐   **2.**   I kept it up for a while, but it fizzled out eventually.

☐   **3.**   I had a great time doing it for years, got really good at it
and met lots of interesting people.

☐   **4.**   I still love doing it and it's a fantastic part of my life.

Now, having filled that out, just notice how you feel.

_____

_____

Do you miss your spark?

_____

_____

Do you remember it with appreciation?

_____

_____

Peter Benson's team researched the concept for almost twenty years. He discovered that:

1. **Every young person understands the idea of spark.**

2. **Kids who have a spark in their life do better at school, are happier, meet and talk to more older people and are more confident and positive. They are more caring, relaxed and sociable, expect the future to be good, and can work harder and understand that good things take time.**

3. **It is even better if kids have more than one spark. In fact, the ability to enthusiastically master an interest area tends to make you try other things as well.**

4. **For a spark to fire up and not go out, it needs two things: at least one adult in the family who is interested and helps make it happen (drives her to harp lesson, buys the aquarium, finds a good dance school) and an adult or two at school or elsewhere who also know about and support it.**

5. **Tragically, a third of kids have no spark alive in them by their late teens. A spark can go out if we don't blow on it.**

THE WIDER BENEFITS

Everyone can understand that an interest area makes a young person happier. But why does it have such a great effect on the other areas of their lives? Why would an interest in tropical fish or surfing make a girl do better at school, be kinder, or believe in the future?

There are a whole bunch of reasons. The first is that when you do an activity you love, you go into a zone. You forget about time. You get so taken up in it that you absolutely relax and are focused and 'in the flow'. *This is good for you.*

Second, almost every interest you care to name involves other people. Often these are people from age groups that kids don't spend a lot of time with these days. Young adults, old people, eccentric and wild and different people. And unlike your peer group, or boring old mum and dad, the people who share passionate interests don't really care about your age, gender, size or shape. They just love to talk and share and teach. There's a massive amount of role-modelling, you catch the enthusiasm of others, learn the attitudes that make things go well, experience more success at trout fishing or orienteering or electronics or fashion design. You feel valued and that you belong, and it's nothing to do with how hot you look or how you style your hair, or how many friends you have on social media. So your social skills grow, you get to be an expert in something, and you wake up in the morning just busting to do it again!

All of the above gains are side effects, which is how almost all the best learning takes place. Babies don't learn to walk or crawl because it's an important milestone. They want to get across that room! It's the results they are interested in. (The terrible trend to testing and performance in education gets this the wrong way round. The message is: 'just practise this maths, memorize this, pass this test, study this, and one day you will get to use it, perhaps'. Nothing is better designed to turn kids off learning than this forced approach.) All real learning, that goes deep and stays, happens because it's useful and fun and makes us feel more alive.

ARE THERE FALSE SPARKS?

In a nutshell, yes. Sometimes girls' interest areas are simply part of the disease of look-ism and performance anxiety that so hampers their lives. Dieting is probably not a great interest area. Exercise – for its own sake or to look buff – poison! Enjoying a sport for the love of it is a totally different thing.

And not all interests fulfil the criteria of 'bridging her to the world'. Computer gaming, while it can be relaxing and stress-busting, easily gets addictive. And it tends to isolate you from real interaction. Some games involve interaction with people elsewhere, but it's pretty limited. It probably needs to be in moderation.

THE GREAT DANCE SCHOOL DISASTER

Dancing is a wonderful thing – it's something that every human culture has done from the beginnings of time. And it seems to be almost embedded in the spirit of girls (and many boys too). When we are happy we just naturally dance about. And the reverse works too – when we dance (even just leaping about in the living room) it makes us feel happier. Dancing can both express and change how you are feeling. After all, emotions are a part of our bodies – we feel with and in our bodies, and when we move, those feelings go where they need to go. It's not just our body that is exercised by dancing, it's our heart, and soul.

Dance is one of the most loved physical activities of childhood. Almost 90 per cent of UK girls go to dance class at some time. But dance isn't immune to some of the larger problems of our culture. That old combination – sexualization and the focus on 'how do I look?' – has put it into the toxic mix. And competitiveness and perfectionism can take away the joy pretty fast, twisting up this previously great part of childhood.

Psychologists treat many dance-obsessed girls who are wracked with body image anxieties, near-anorexic eating patterns, very negative self-talk, and borderline self-harming routines of exercise and overtraining. And they were in a dance school culture which fostered these attitudes, and was making them worse. Add to that the new aspect of having to dance in sexual ways when you are only five, and clothing designed to add to that, and it's a fairly harmful scene.

But Change Is Coming

A group of young dance teachers in Australia recently started a national campaign to get dance back on track. They created a code of conduct, along with an accreditation for child-friendly dance schools. (You can learn about the code at www.kidspacecode.com.)

Some of the key things to look for are:

- Costumes – are they appropriate for the age of the children?

- The actual dance routines – ditto.

- Lyrics and song choices – ditto.

- Fat-shaming do teachers directly or indirectly make girls feel bad for not conforming to a certain shape?

- Overly competitive and judgemental, joy-killing attitudes to what is supposed to be fun.

In a nutshell, six-year-old girls twerking and hip-thrusting, making eyes, pouting and wearing false eyelashes, to a lyric like 'Give it to me, it makes me feel so good' while a hard-faced teacher yells at them to lose weight, work harder, and practise till they drop maybe isn't a good idea.

So, here is a quick evaluation.

Has your daughter ever learned dance?

☐ YES   ☐ NO

Did she enjoy it?

☐ YES   ☐ NO

Were the costumes, music and styles of dancing age-appropriate?

☐ YES   ☐ NO (they were very adultified)

Was there a lot of pressure and angst about doing it right?

☐ YES   ☐ SOME   ☐ NO

Was the dancing ever individual, expressive, joyful and spontaneous?

(or was it always about routines, performance, and dancing as you were told?)

☐ YES   ☐ NO

_____

_____

_____

Dance isn't the only problem area – any sport or athletic pursuit can go overboard. A few years ago the Australian women's gymnastics team, made up mostly of teenagers, was investigated in a Senate Enquiry after many of the girls ceased menstruating and their growth hormone levels dipped below what was expected, affecting their eventual height and possibly their reproductive organ formation. Overtraining was suspected to be the cause of these really major health issues.

Cessation of periods from overtraining also leads to hormonal changes which can cause osteoporosis – bone weakening, also with lifelong effects. And there is just the stress of all that practice and the continual fear of failure.

Competition is healthy, but only up to a point. When it gets out of hand, then your daughter is just an object to achieve someone else's goals. Make sure that someone else isn't you.

Tick the statements which are true for your girl:

☐ 1. The activities my daughter participates in are just for fun and enjoyment, and they really make her happy.

☐ 2. Sometimes her activities stress her, or cause her physical overload.

☐ 3. What she is learning is hard, but it's teaching her grit, and she is getting a lot from it.

☐ 4. She likes her activities, but there are just too many of them. We might have to cut back.

☐ 5. I think we'd better quit that activity. It's totally doing her more harm than good.

LIFE IS FOR THRIVING – NOT JUST SURVIVING

Sometimes we fall into a terrible trap as parents. We develop a negative orientation, or at least a not-very-ambitious one – of just getting through. When life is hard, it's easy to do this – focus on the negatives, and not aim any higher. We only seek to keep them fed, keep them out of trouble, keep them in school. These are important, but they are 'management and control' issues.

If you find yourself living in 'survival mode' rather than really having a happy life, it's important to ask a bigger, better question – 'what would help our family really thrive and be happy'? Peter Benson found that about a quarter of parents focused on 'thriving'. They wanted their children to really feel alive.

This starts with re-evaluating your goals. So, to begin with, ask: 'What is my highest aspiration for my child?' Have a think about it for a minute, and see what you come up with. Peter suggests that very few would answer 'achieve the national benchmark in maths' or 'fall in the top percentile of GCSE scores' or 'win Olympic Gold'. Even 'be rich and successful' doesn't get many votes, if we really think about it – because that's not a recipe for happiness.

Far more of us would answer with things like:

- **Experience joy**

- **Be connected and engaged**

- **Fall in love with life**

- **Be generous, contributing, happy and kind**

This is the language of thriving – of quality, not quantity. And if that's what we aspire to, then we have to check whether this what we really convey to our kids, day to day. Deep down, we can want really worthwhile things for our kids as they grow up. But in practice, it comes across more as 'compete, win, be afraid'. Those are surefire recipes for being lonely, empty, medicated, confused or lost.

It's a delicate thing, giving our kids enough space and time to find what they really love to do. I suspect that this does not mean crowding their spare time with lots of classes, sports and commitments. Or flitting from one to another. It's more patient, perhaps even a little boring, to allow their own inner confidence to emerge. Our job is to notice the interest, to let them know that we 'see' them, and are happy to support them in that pursuit.

Schools Can Help

Schools have a big role in spark maintenance. Benson believes that a child's teacher ought to be aware of the sparks of each of the children in their class. That it's the first thing to be discussed at parent teacher nights, since unless a teacher knows where the child's passions lie, how can they form a real connection? Local councils should survey the sparks of their young people, and see how well they match the kind of facilities they provide.

It's a delicate thing,
giving our kids enough space
and time to find what they
really love to do.

In almost every case, a young person's spark is something good, beautiful and useful to the world. We shouldn't worry about 'where will this lead?' or 'how will they make a living?' because human development is not about end goals, but about *getting this stage right*. It's about right now, doing what you feel called to. Your mind, body and soul know what they need to do next. And that will unfold. You can trust human development, it's been going on for a very long time.

Benson found that about half of the young people he studied found a career that was related to their spark – the others kept their spark as something that refreshed and renewed them while doing a different kind of job. And that was OK.

When do you feel best, most full of life?

Talk about spark with your daughter – what do you feel most alive doing? Talk about the obstacles to following her spark. Who does she know that has a really evident spark? Tell her about your own.

Have a spark dialogue that is ongoing in your family's conversations. If you have been feeling a bit cut off from your girl – if you work long hours, for example – then this can be a way back to connection with her.

As a final thing – we adults, too, need to have a spark. We need that aliveness and sense of being our own self, even amidst the demands of looking after other little lives. See if you can get your spark back!

Spark

In a Nutshell

Every young person has a spark or two.

These are the things inside them that they would just love to do.

Sparks thrive when adults both in the family and outside the family support and help them along.

Tragically too many kids (and adults) lose their spark.

Our job is to help our kids find their spark, and help them pursue it.

A kid with a strong interest area does better in almost every aspect of their life.

Beware of activities that are too competitive, or driven, or based on being perfect. If it's a true spark, it will be energizing and fun.

Chapter Six

Aunties

" One of the great secrets of wellbeing for girls is the presence of aunties. Especially at puberty. "

A CIRCLE OF WOMEN

Erin's mother had been very sick for a long time, and Erin had known for months that she would die. But really, nothing can prepare you at twelve years of age for losing your mum. The day of the funeral went OK – in fact, if she was honest, preparing for it and getting through it had given them all something to focus on. But as they filed out into the church foyer, and people began to group together and talk, a cloak of self-protective numbness seemed to settle on her shoulders. As if it was all a dream. But she knew it wasn't – it was a nightmare she couldn't ever wake from. Her gentle, wise mother was gone.

She watched as people gathered around her dad. He had an arm around her younger brother Mikey, keeping him close. That morning he'd told her she shouldn't feel obliged to talk to people after the service, that it was OK to do whatever she needed. She backed up against a wall, alone, and hoped no-one would notice her.

All at once, there was someone at her side. It was Tania, her mum's best friend, who she liked a lot – they were in and out of each other's houses all the time. Tania was looking at her oddly: 'Erin, can I borrow you for a minute?' She couldn't really think of an answer, perhaps they needed help in the kitchen was the thought that first came into her head. They went around a corner, down a corridor and into a smaller room. Then she saw them. Five or six women, standing, clearly waiting for her. No dishes in sight.

Her auntie Margaret, down from the country, and others she knew, Mum's jogging friends, and frequent visitors to their house on and off. She knew their names, and a little about each of them. They were all looking straight at her. Sandy, the oldest, silver-haired, spoke first.

'Listen, honey, this is a tough day, you just want to get through it, I know. But we wanted to get you in here to let you know something. We aren't going anywhere. We loved your mum and we love you too. We plan to stay in your face, whatever you need.'

Sandy looked kind of stern, but had tears in her eyes, and suddenly Erin, though she had vowed not to, knew she was going to start crying too. She felt the women draw closer and those beside her put their arms around her, just gently, respectfully. She crumpled, not even knowing who it was, into the nearest chest, and was enfolded, and a wailing sound came from deep inside her and she just let it go. Gradually, she just felt their warm bodies close to her, wanting to stay there forever, breathing their scent. The small, glimmering possibility hit her, that perhaps, after all, she could survive.

WHAT EVERY GIRL NEEDS

Girls need aunties or auntie figures if they are to make it to womanhood intact. There are reasons for this that lie deep in our prehistory – as hunter-gatherers, we always lived in close-knit family clans where the women surrounded the girls with teaching and support, for the big transitions as well as the day-to-day details of life. The care of the girls was a sacred duty. And remember – those cultures were matriarchal – you didn't mess with the women.

How we live has changed, but our psychology hasn't. Girls are designed with a need for more than just mum. Luckily, this isn't too hard, since loving women naturally want to help the girls they know to grow up safe and well.

Aunties are great when you are little, but it's in the teen years that they become crucial. There are times when a girl doesn't want to talk to her mum. Or is in conflict with her mum. And there is an age – around fourteen or fifteen – when a girl only knows one thing for sure, that she doesn't want to turn out like her mum. Don't feel bad – that's true even if mum is a prime minister or a rock star. It's hard not to feel wounded when she goes through this phase, but be assured it's only short term. And it's necessary – it's the booster rocket that fires her off from the mother ship to become her own person. A little overreaction is needed, or she would never 'individuate' (or move out of the house, eventually!). That and the intense irritatingness of fathers, which is a whole different subject.

So in the mid-teens – especially – *girls need someone else*. If there is no auntie or no other wise women in her everyday life, then she has to settle for the next best thing. She defaults to the peer group – other girls – for her wisdom, perspective, nurture and balance.

Peer groups are for fun and companionship. But they don't yet have the skills or knowledge to be of real support. It's one of the most poignant things on earth to see kids trying to help each other through the terrible things that can happen in their lives, when the adults aren't up to the job. (When one girl I know was in Year 12, she and her friends brought food for a girl whose mum was just too preoccupied with her own affairs – literally – to have anything in the fridge.) But depending on your peers for mentoring is way too fraught. Peer groups tend to make each other more anxious, not less. And girls of the same age are competitors, and not always to be trusted.

Girls need, and in the past always had – wise, cool, feisty, tough-minded aunties to do four things – confront them, comfort them, praise them and challenge them. Aunties ask the big questions. Mothers ask: 'Have you got clean undies?' Aunties ask: 'What do you want your life to be about? What's important to you? What do you stand for?' They ask how your life is going just as your mum does, but you feel that you can tell them because they won't get so anxious that they just make matters worse.

As well as this, aunties also talk tough, and people who love us but talk tough to us get into our heads in a very interesting way. I have known many young women who, in a fit of rebellious anger at their parents, at life, at the world, were on the brink of a self-destructive act. Getting into a car with drunken boys they had only met that night. Taking a pill given to them by a stranger at a party. Walking home without asking friends to go with

them at 3 a.m. (Yes, I know a woman's place is everywhere, reclaim the streets, but it's still dumb.) Driving their own car drunk and angry at a broken heart, feeling like life is over. But as they went to do this, they had a picture of their auntie in their heads with the most angry look you can imagine. Like, 'ARE YOU STUPID?!' And they quietly said no and turned and walked away. Aunties can save your life without even being around.

The other thing aunties talk a lot of sense about is boys and men. They aren't even faintly impressed by the male gender (this may be why single aunties have a lot of appeal). They say things like: 'He may be pretty, but there's nothing between the ears, honey! He'll bore the tits off you after half an hour!' And other things which I can't write here, but you get the idea. Aunties talk you out of worrying what boys think. They teach you how to manage them. How to spot the ones worth caring about. How to spot the jerks. Invaluable stuff.

HOW TO BE AN AUNTIE

So here's how you do it. When they are about eight years old, have them over to your house to stay a night, or two. Sleeping safe and welcome in your auntie's house does something deep and primal to a girl. Do it when your husband or sons are away, if it makes it more quiet and safe for her. She has another home. She begins to see she has independence, the world has other welcomes.

When she is going through puberty, let her know you know. Tell her how great it is. (See the big section further on about this.) When she is a teenager, have regular – perhaps monthly –

lunches out with her to keep tabs on her world. Perhaps there will be something she really needs to tell someone, that she can't tell mum. It could be huge – that her stepfather is starting to touch her in a way that makes her uncomfortable. That she is starting to notice that her sexuality is not the generic one. Or it could be more everyday – that she is worried about her parents, or a friend, or a dilemma of her own. There will be loads to talk about that is lighthearted too. An auntie is someone less worried, more adventurous, more raunchy, more mischievous than her mum. She's fun.

All this said, don't compete with or try to usurp her mum. Admire her mum in front of her. You are only a visiting resource, not a co-mother. A fairy godmother. Don't spend lavishly on her, at least, not often. But your time, classiness and a feeling of being grown up will all encourage the same in her.

You don't have to be an auntie to do auntie-ing. It can arise just from being close to the family and finding that your heart feels a connection. As we said at the start, it's an ancient role and women just naturally slide into it. It requires a lightness of touch. But an absolute sense that you are rock solid. You will be there for her.

Your own daughters will need aunties too. Perhaps it will be a reciprocal arrangement! It's OK to ask one of your sisters: 'Can you auntie my girl?' It might be specific: 'Something is worrying her, she isn't right – could you have a talk to her?' Girls are very perceptive, though, so be subtle. Long-term involvement is the best.

And in case this all sounds a bit hard – excuse my male awkwardness. I am sure you will know what to do. And, of course, the main reason for being around young people is that they are a hoot! You will have a great time.

So here's the interactive part, though you hardly need it.

1. Were aunties important in your growing up?

☐ YES   ☐ A BIT   ☐ NO

If they were, what was it that they did that was right for you?

_____

_____

If there were none, do you think it could have made a difference? What might have changed in your life, had there been someone you could tell anything to, who was kind, understanding and wise?

_____

_____

2. Have you got nieces? Or daughters of friends whom you love?

☐ YES   ☐ NO

If yes, could you see yourself playing a greater part in their life?

☐ YES   ☐ A BIT   ☐ NO (of course, distance is a factor too).

3. Do you think your daughter would benefit from an auntie or auntie figure in her life?

☐ YES   ☐ A BIT   ☐ NO   ☐ SHE ALREADY HAS A GREAT ONE (OR TWO)

4. Could you possibly recruit suitable family or friends for the role?

☐ YES   ☐ PERHAPS   ☐ NO

Aunties talk tough

PUBERTY AND GIRLS – HOW TO MAKE IT GREAT

Boys and girls do puberty very differently. Girls shoot up in height, boys catch up slow. Girls start at least a year sooner, often more. In boys, puberty is gradual – and we have some time to get used to it. But with girls there is one change that is not gradual at all. Suddenly, one day they get a period – and there you are. They are fertile. They are women. This makes it all rather intense. How this can be handled really well, and the opportunities to make the time of turning into a woman really special, will make up the rest of this chapter. Mothers involved in testing this book found this to be one of the most exciting and helpful sections and made many plans to incorporate it into their daughter's growing up. I hope you will too.

THE BAD OLD DAYS

In the twentieth century, having your first period was treated as just an embarrassing hygiene problem. Many mothers reading this will have had less than ideal experiences with their own first periods arriving, and how this was handled.

Please tick the item below that best describes how your parents handled helping you with your first period:

☐ 1. It was awful, misinformed and embarrassing.

☐ 2. It was OK but mostly about the practicalities, not anything special about womanhood or the good meanings of it all.

☐ 3. It was fine really, my parents were good and I felt OK.

☐ 4. It was a very special time, my mum and I got closer, and I felt grown up and excited to be entering womanhood.

Answering those questions, you'll be aware of feelings that are bad, good, or mixed, around this subject. You will be able to locate those feelings as actual sensations in your body that come up just because we've raised the topic. Just stop for a second and notice – where in your body do those sensations reside? It's good to notice those sensations, and let them shift as you decide – we can do this really well, using much better help that wasn't always available back then.

KIM McCABE

Kim has been a youthworker specializing in sexuality education, parenting girls, and child psychology for over twenty years. She is the founder of Rites for Girls, which trains practitioners across the UK in delivering rite-of-passage programmes and support groups. She is the author of a new book on this topic, *The Emerging Woman*, and her website **www.ritesforgirls.com** is the focus for a growing community of parents and educators worldwide, and a great source for resources and ideas.

Because girls' puberty is clearly a women's domain, I enlisted the help of Kim McCabe. Kim is a good friend who works with early teenage girls in Sussex, England, and has long experience in youth work and education. Kim pioneered working with girls entering puberty in year-long small support groups, which aim to make the puberty year a great and life-affirming time for them and their parents. Girls and their mothers totally love these groups, and Kim now trains others to do the same. What follows are for the most part Kim's words, and so please read on in a female voice!

First Blood

When your daughter bleeds for the first time this marks a huge change – she can now conceive, carry and bear a child. She joins the worldwide sisterhood of fertile women. It's a huge step on her journey toward womanhood.

For many girls this is an intensely private event and not something they would want to broadcast. You might be required to respect her wish for privacy, even though you may be bursting with feelings such as excitement, joy and sadness.

Our first bleed is a threshold experience – in a single moment we pass through a gateway. Most women clearly remember their first time, usually with a mixture of feelings. How did you feel? What was special about it for you? How would you have liked it to be different? Who did you tell? How did they respond?

The experience of a first period, coming as it does at a time of great hormonal change, can vary enormously from one girl to another. For some it is a long awaited marker of a new and special status. For others it can be a dreaded and embarrassing event. Some feel quietly, privately special. Some feel full of fear and overwhelmed. Some struggle with mood swings, cramps and bloating. Others cannot understand what all the fuss is about.

Your daughter will handle her first time so much better if you have prepared her by talking comfortably to her about menstruation while she was growing up. Unless we talk openly, we risk our girls being uneducated, misinformed, ashamed, awkward or afraid. The suicide helpline The Samaritans was set up in 1953 after the death of a fourteen-year-old girl. She had started her periods, but having no one to talk to believed that she had a sexually transmitted disease and took her own life. And yes – even today – some mothers neglect to raise the subject.

The Practical Stuff

Make sure your daughter knows what to do when she first starts bleeding. She may not be at home, or may not want to involve anyone when it begins. So:

- **Does she know her options (pads, tampons), where to find them and how to use them?**

- **Does she know that rolled-up toilet paper can do the job if she has nothing else to hand?**

- **Does she know how to wash blood from her clothing?**

Let your daughter know that sometimes a girl can have a first period, and then go for a few months before having another, or have the next one just a few weeks later. It takes a while to settle into a monthly rhythm. Let her know this is normal, and not to worry. It is also increasingly common for girls to suffer cramping during their first few periods, so reassure her that they won't always be this way.

If intense cramping goes on for more than a few months it may indicate an imbalance and it's worth seeking professional help from a naturopath or doctor.

There are feelings to talk about too:

- **Explain that during your period, it is natural to feel strong emotions – and that she doesn't have to bottle them up.**

- **Explain that the first sight of blood can be startling, both because of what it signifies, and because at any other time blood indicates injury and pain.**

- **Share with your daughter in a good-humoured way your experiences of mood swings, PMT, sugar cravings, etc., and also how you manage them.**

- **Make sure, without sounding heavy or judgemental, that she knows that she can become pregnant now – even when she is bleeding, even if it is her first time.**

It's never too late, even if she is menstruating already, to talk about all these things. Girls are hungry to know that they're normal, that periods are not something that need to be hidden, that you are there to support them.

Start young, long before it's an issue, to normalize it all. Take advantage of when the issues are raised on television, on the radio or in the newspapers and talk about it that way. Find a book. Use humour. Have a giggle.

When the Time Comes, Make It Special

When your daughter starts to bleed, or when she tells you that she has started, mark the specialness of the event – but tread carefully, you are on sacred ground, and your daughter requires sensitivity and respect.

Do something to make it special. This can have several ingredients. Often a special gift is appropriate, a keepsake or memento. A heartfelt letter that says more than you could say out loud. A trip or shared experience. You might include something daring and unusual that you do together, like a naked swim in a lake! Even if this is just something the two of you do, it sends a strong message:

As your mum, I welcome you to womanhood.
I see you as a new person now, more of an equal.
I want you to love being a woman, from the very first.
This is an important milestone, and I celebrate you reaching it.

WHAT IS A RITE OF PASSAGE?

Just doing the aforementioned things may be quite enough for you. But we wanted to open up another possibility – of doing something that involves others, especially the women in her life that matter to her and can help her. This was what human communities have been doing since time immemorial. A rite of passage is a way of saying: 'We see you, we support you, we acknowledge that you are growing up and can begin to shoulder responsibility for your own life and we expect you to do so.'

There is a very compelling reason to do this. If we don't give them some formal marker of reaching adulthood, *young people will create their own*. And tragically, it's often through the use of drugs, alcohol, fast cars, sex or teenage pregnancy. A remarkable amount of teenage risk-taking behaviour is their own clumsy attempt at self-initiation. Offering something better can change their life, or even save their life. It really matters.

How It Works

Moving from the child stage to the adult stage in life means great changes in the psyche. A significant shift is required to move from girl to woman psychology, and if we create an event to mark this, it is less likely for a girl to grow up into a woman-child and more likely for her to become a grown woman of vision. It is stressful to live an adult life and yet have the psychology of a child – although many do. Far better that we invest energy into the maturation process, giving our girls a sense of what it is to be a woman and guide their journey of becoming one.

Creating a Rite of Passage

A rite of passage can be as involved as the other rites (marriage, christening, funeral) or it can be delightfully simple. A ritual does not have to be out in the woods, with candles and chanting and what many a teenager would deem to be 'weirdness'!

A ritual can be normal and special at the same time. It can be meaningful without having to include things that would make your daughter cringe. Teenagers are notoriously easy to embarrass, and sensitivity to this is essential in allowing her to be fully present at her own event. Equally, magic happens – in the right setting, people will suddenly feel moved to say or do things that are important and special which surprise even them. Trust that, if you keep it simple and sincere, it will be powerful. Whether you design something for her yourself, or you and your daughter create something together, it is important to tailor her rite of passage to suit her. You are looking for a balance between comfort and challenge. Both are needed.

Involving Significant Women

There are three options of how to go about doing a rite of passage for your girl becoming a woman. The first, and simplest, is to just involve you and her, as we have described above.

The second is to involve a group of women who love and care about your daughter. To me, this is the most powerful, and wonderful option, as it so strongly tells her of her worth. She cannot but be moved and affected, and everyone involved will feel that power of commitment.

Or you might decide as a group of mothers to work together to create something for all your girls of around the same puberty age. But having something just for her is especially powerful, because this so rarely happens for our daughters these days. The meaning will be 'full strength' and being the only 'new woman' among 'old women' has a gravity and power that will change her deeply.

Allow your intuition to guide you towards what would be right for your daughter. Talk it over with older women in your family, close women friends, other young women that you know; but start with you first. Trust that your knowledge of your daughter will help suggest to you what might serve her best as a way of honouring her emerging womanhood.

PLANNING THE EVENT

- Begin by thinking about what gives her pleasure – go to her comfort zone first.

- What is important to her – what would give this meaning?

- Then consider what might take her to an edge – just out of her comfort zone.

- Think about who could be supportive to her in this.

- Who are the important females in her life – who else could be involved or invited?

- Who will lead the ritual – you, a friend, a family member, a celebrant?

- What could you do that would make her feel special?

- Would some element of surprise serve to heighten the experience – an unexpected guest, an extra challenge, some words from a grandmother, something hand-made for her?

- What is the most suitable venue – comfortable, private, special?

- A word about taking photographs: although it can be lovely to have a visual record of the event, recording the event can interfere with the experience. So decide beforehand what you want and communicate this clearly to everyone present. We suggest not having photographs until the process is ended, then taking some celebratory ones showing all present.

All rituals need a beginning, a happening and an end, followed by feasting. This can be as simple as lighting a candle, speaking, blowing the candle out and sharing a hot chocolate. It can also involve a lot more.

How It Works

The Welcome

Put folks at their ease by welcoming them, perhaps remembering those who cannot be there, saying what you are gathered for (to mark your daughter's stepping away from childhood and towards adulthood) and explaining what is going to happen. You may want to say more about what you and your daughter have done to get to this point. People will appreciate being told what is going to be expected of them. Physical contact can help to bring intimacy to the gathering. Although often spontaneous, it can also set the tone, as long as it feels comfortable: holding hands, washing your daughter's feet or hands, massaging feet or hands, a hug, a kiss, placing hands on her head.

The Happening

This is where you do something that gives meaning and purpose to the event. The possibilities for what you do are infinite. Your daughter may have prepared something for this part of the ceremony. She may have an intention or vow for herself that she would like to speak aloud. You may have given her a challenge to perform. You may have asked others close to your daughter to participate in some way.

Blessings and Offerings

Words spoken in a ritual setting carry great weight. This can be a good time to offer words of support, words of acknowledgement of a girl's skills and strengths, words of warning, and words of wisdom.

The Symbolic Gift

Give your daughter a gift to symbolize and acknowledge her achievement – to serve as a talisman and to remind her of the power of what she has undergone. The time and thought that you give to the choice of gift is more powerful than its cost.

Gift ideas: A hand-made purse filled with treasures; a piece of family jewellery; a heart-shaped stone; a letter written from the heart; some significant trinket from your past; a poem; a tree planted somewhere special; a family heirloom; something home-made; a box.

Closing

It is important to let people know when the ceremony is ended. Thank them for being there. Blow out a candle, blow your daughter a kiss, clap, hug, sing her name, shout three cheers, whatever seems right.

Merry-making

Finish with a celebration – feasting on favourite foods, special people, music, merry-making. Some would say there must be dancing! Or music at least, or singing.

Do you feel that you would like to create a special event for your daughter when she 'comes of age' as a woman?

☐ YES

☐ PERHAPS

☐ NO

Would you like to enlist the help of other women in her life?

☐ YES

☐ NO

Are you looking forward to this time as a real milestone in your life as a parent?

☐ YES

☐ YES, BUT WITH TREPIDATION

☐ NO, TERRIFIED!

I hope it's a yes. But if not, that you gain the confidence by the time it arrives!

'She cannot
but be moved
and affected,
and everyone
involved
will feel that
power of
commitment.'

DADS, DAUGHTERS AND BOUNDARIES

Because dads are the opposite sex to daughters, it's important to be sensitive about your daughter's privacy boundaries. Respect her space! Daughters from early puberty onwards, but sometimes younger, can become intensely private. So even though your family may have been quite relaxed and natural about bodies and showered with children, for example, when they were young, things can change when they get a bit older.

Here are some guidelines:

1. **Don't just barge into the bathroom when she is in there.**

2. **Always knock at her bedroom door and, in general, don't enter unless invited. It's important for a girl to know she has a safe and private space.**

3. **Sense when you go to hug or embrace her whether she moves into that touch, or tenses up or withdraws. She may do different things at different times.**

4. **If as a parent you feel worried about something and feel you need to check in her room, always have her mother do that. Girls may feel intruded on by their mother, and mildly annoyed, but feel violated and betrayed if it is their father doing that same thing.**

5. **If you are a single dad, it's fine to talk about girl stuff with your daughter, and she may be happy to do so. But you may sense that she feels more comfortable if you involve a woman she trusts, an auntie or grandma. Let her decide.**

In the bad old days, fathers often felt they should not touch their daughters at all, or especially as they approached puberty. Many women I have asked about this talk sadly about their dads getting awkward and distant with them as they entered their teens. She can feel that there is something wrong with her, that you don't like her any more, or that you don't like the fact she is growing up. It's important to still be affectionate with our daughters as long as that's what they want and seem to seek out. By being sensitive to whether she likes it or not, just as with anyone else, we can continue to show warmth and affection to girls, and boys, at every age.

Aunties

In a Nutshell

 Aunties are an ancient and essential part of helping girls grow up, especially in the teenage years, though it begins much sooner.

Aunties are an ancient and essential part of helping girls grow up, especially in the teenage years, though it begins much sooner.

A rite of passage helps a girl have a positive and liberating passage through puberty. Creating an event, especially if you involve the significant women in her life, can be a moving introduction to womanhood, and literally grow her up.

Chapter Seven

A Happy Sexuality

> Many things in the world are getting better for girls. But sex isn't one of them. We still don't give girls enough positive messages about how great it can be. And the porn explosion is miseducating boys with violent and depersonalized ideas about how sex works. Girls need to know that they deserve better — and boys need to be better taught.

Abby broke off the kiss with a smile, it was like coming up for air. Luke's face stayed close to hers, his eyes cast downwards – his forehead nuzzled hers gently. They were both sixteen and saw each other almost every day. Sometimes talking over things that were going on in their lives, other times just lost in the delight of holding each other close. And those kisses.

He never pushed her for more, and that was one reason why she liked him so much, felt so easy being close to him. Sometimes she would have liked more, but it just felt best where things were uncomplicated. She would have given a boy who tried to force things pretty short shrift; in fact she had done that with boys in the past. She didn't want to be the sex-police. She wanted someone who would meet her where she was.

When she chose to have sex for the first time, it would be amazing, she knew, if this was anything to go by. Something inside her told her that time was not yet. And she trusted herself to know.

It says something important that for many of us – especially dads – thinking of our daughters as sexual is something we'd rather not do! It's always been an area that is somewhat fraught and full of risk. What a shame that is! If we can't think about it, then how can we talk about it? And if we can't talk about it, how can we help them? This chapter will help with that.

In the area of sexuality, most of us parents have two goals. We want our kids to grow into adults who have happy love lives, exciting, trusting and close. And secondly, we want the journey to that destination to take place slowly (we would probably choose VERY slowly!) and safely, without too much pain or disappointment. And certainly no exploitation. We've survived adolescence ourselves – we know the dangers, the dark side of sex, as well as its joys.

Today the dark side is uppermost. Everyone involved with young people around the world is seeing a sudden and disturbing trend towards unhappy and damaging sexual experiences. The cause is not hard to find. The arrival of online pornography and its wide use by young people, especially boys, is miseducating a generation about how sex works. And since we still don't always do sex education well in schools, and find it a difficult topic at home, the incredibly negative effects of porn aren't being properly countered.

Luckily a lot is being learned about how we can help. Young people are actually hungry for guidance, however cool or shut down they may appear. They need our monitoring and boundary setting because their brains are often too immature to choose well. And they need above all to be able to talk freely, think things through, and know that we have a very positive view of love and sex. Girls who have open and informative relationships with the adults in their lives wait longer, choose better and have far happier times.

This chapter matters whatever age your daughter is, because sexuality is about lifelong learning. Teaching our daughters that:

1. **Sex is good**
2. **Her body is hers**
3. **She deserves to enjoy and be free in how she loves**

A VOICE IN THE WILDERNESS

Melinda Tankard Reist is standing before an audience of two hundred girls aged from twelve to eighteen. Neat in their school uniforms, they are seated in curved rows on the floor. Uncharacteristically for this age group, they are utterly silent. Melinda is the founder of Collective Shout, a national network of young women campaigners against the sexual exploitation of women and girls. She will criss-cross to schools across the country giving this talk about 'sex, porn and love' dozens of times a year to girls of every ethnicity and demographic. When Melinda finishes speaking, the girls erupt in applause and besiege her with tearful thanks for her message. They will tell stories of their own experience – of being touched or assaulted by boys or men on public transport, of being leered at or spoken to obscenely in the schoolyard. Or, in their relationships with boyfriends, of feeling pressured into doing things they didn't want to do, and of sexual encounters entered into happily and trustingly, where nice boys that they thought they could trust became aggressive, spoke demeaningly or physically hurt them.

When Melinda talks to boys about these issues, they often express shame and regret, recognizing they have acted in these ways, but not seeing how harmful and disrespectful their behaviour has been. They literally thought this was how you were supposed to treat girls.

The world our kids grow up in today sexually is not a happy place. Sex has been so misused, in advertising, the media and in music videos – and most powerfully of all in the torrent of online pornography – that it has badly distorted what young people think about how it works, and how it can be part of a caring, gradually unfolding relationship.

A recent study by the Burnet Institute in Sydney, Australia, found that 90 per cent of boys and 60 per cent of girls had encountered pornography between the ages of thirteen and sixteen. Thirteen was the average age of first exposure for boys. Forty-four per cent of older teenage boys watch porn weekly, and 37 per cent daily. This indicates a fair bit of exposure. Pornography is a vast and highly profitable industry. Our consumer society is industrializing sexuality, and the kids are its first trial run.

A generation ago, boys sneaked a look at photos of dewy-eyed girls on satin sheets in *Playboy*. Today it is very different. One study found that 88 per cent of porn depicts violence towards women. Over 50 per cent includes verbal abuse. Defenders of pornography argue that much of this is simply BDSM material, which is consensual, but I am not sure if mid-adolescent boys understand this or benefit from seeing it. Crucially, for the boys who see these depictions, the women in pornography are paid to act as if they like and enjoy this treatment – slapping, strangling, hair-pulling, and being called abusive and demeaning names. For a fourteen-year-old boy the mislearning about what sex is like is bewildering, if not dangerous.

Thankfully not every boy is exposed to the same degree – if his parents monitor his online time the exposure will be much less. And not every boy succumbs to the message. But it cannot fail to create a conflict in his mind between the empathy and kindness he has learned in childhood and the message about how to treat women that he sees enacted on the screen. His brain is being altered. It is hard to unsee what one has seen or keep it from intruding into consciousness when in the company of real live girls.

WHY HAS PORN BECOME VIOLENT?

Men and boys are human beings – they too have the oxytocin release in sex that promotes tenderness and bonding. They too crave affection, trust and passion, but the photographs and movies don't love you back. Seconds after using porn, the user feels empty and flat. The good feeling doesn't arrive as it would from lying warmly in the arms of someone who cares for you. And also, the endorphin flow from even raw sexual excitement of watching porn quickly habituates, so ordinary porn rapidly loses impact. Only novelty can bring it back and so, next time, they need more – more severe, explicit, 'hard core' and, inevitably, more violent – in order to be aroused. What some boys end up watching is too sickening to describe here.

There are dangerous side effects to this. The cognitive dissonance of a woman being abused on the screen is resolved by the decision that she must deserve it. Empathy dies and misogyny grows. It's a kind of zombie, dead-eyed way of being in the world where sex is separated from anything relational. Boys addicted to pornography grow less capable of relating to real girls.

For those of us who remember working for sexual freedom and openness, seeing the charnel-house this has led to is sobering. Calls for the restriction or banning of pornography that would have been scorned a few years ago are now being seriously debated, impossible though it might be to achieve. We ban child pornography and it may well be that restrictions on violent 'erotica' will have to come too. Just having to prove you are adult would be an important first step.

But back to our girls. How do we address this with those entering their teens in this dark time?

Here is what Melinda (and educators like her) report from talking to adolescent girls:

1. **They are being increasingly and persistently pressured into sexual acts that they don't want or enjoy. This pressure often becomes the central focus of the relationship with boys who they thought liked them or wanted to be with them.**

2. **When once teenagers enjoyed hours of kissing, or had a relationship consisting of talking, laughing, spending time together and snogging, this now doesn't happen at all. It's too much a delay in getting to the goal.**

3. **Sex isn't really sexy any more. There is no sensuality, no body pleasure, no tenderness. You are meat to be used. The sex girls have with boys is fourth rate.**

4. **As a result, by sixteen or seventeen, girls are often totally disillusioned about sex, put off it by the dismal lack of skill, awareness or connection offered by the boys in their lives. It becomes a routine, dreary chore to put up with if you want to be in the company of a male. (How progressive and modern!)**

5. **Sexual relationships that start at fourteen or fifteen rarely last beyond a few weeks, often less. They create a lowered bar, a kind of resignation, and drift into multiple, equally empty relationships.**

This doesn't just affect the girls who are sexually active. The effect on the social world that all our daughters move in – at school, university or going out in public on the street – is that it is constantly sexualized in an invasive and uncomfortable way. A girl finds she is being ranked and compared on sexual criteria on social media or even to her face. Some boys feel that they are entitled to touch or grope girls, harass them or worse. Some men gaze invasively at girls without any sense of respect or protectiveness.

Girls lose a sense of agency or that their needs matter. Melinda hears girls talk about their first sexual experience, being anxious only about how it was for the boy. 'He seemed to like it.' 'I hope I looked OK.' There is nothing about their own enjoyment.

By mid-secondary school, requests for naked 'selfies' come thick and fast. Boys expect this from a girl they are friends with. Girls ask: 'How can I refuse without hurting his feelings?' But those photos may be traded among boys, used as revenge, or to blackmail them into having sex, then shared anyway. Girls in many countries have taken their own lives because of the humiliation or betrayal they experience, the sense of having their selves taken away.

Another sad side effect, is that non-sexual, actual friendships – once a great part of being young, and a stepping stone to greater confidence – have almost disappeared as everyone thinks they are supposed to be sexual.

SO WHAT TO DO?

In the face of this avalanche of hurt, the answer that educators and activists are giving girls is on multiple fronts, but has a central core. It's the thing that sends girls at Melinda's talks into empowered assertion of their own feelings. You Don't Have To. Your own sexual wishes, enjoyment, values, and choices, are what you have a right to stand up for. You aren't in this world to satisfy boys.

It's important to be clear here – this isn't about preaching abstinence, or girls being the moral guardian. That has been a spectacular failure. It's about saying: sex is great, and you are in charge of what you want to do, when and who with.

It's shocking that girls even need to be told that.

Positive Messages Do the Most Good

American educator Peggy Orenstein, who has been writing about girls' and women's lives for twenty years, released her book *Girls and Sex* to remarkable acclaim in 2016. Her argument won immediate support for its practicality.

What Orenstein found was that (especially in the US) sex education for girls was seriously deficient. It wasn't that it was wrong, but that it focused on the wrong things. The teaching in schools was all about damage control. Don't get pregnant, don't get sexually transmitted diseases. Those weird diagrams with the ovaries and fallopian tubes like cow horns, and some giggly stuff about condoms. Any questions? No?

What was missing was the *emotions*. And the most important thing of all – *how great it could be*. You can understand why educators, who had fought for almost a century to even give girls the

facts at all, were holding back on enthusing about sex, but that was what was needed. Because the evidence is strong and clear – girls whose mums, aunties, teachers or role models teach them that sex is fantastic, melting, intense, important and lovely, and here's how to make sure it is that way for you too, have the best time of all.

These women raise girls who do three things:

1. **Delay (rather than rush into) their early sexual experiences, often by several years.**

2. **Are much more choosy about who they have even semi-sexual experiences with.**

3. **Get the conditions and circumstances that they want for lovemaking, which usually means without drunkenness and uncertainty. And they experience it as wonderful.**

In short, they take back the power over their bodies and, not surprisingly, things go rather well. Isn't that what you would want for your girl?

HOW WAS IT FOR YOU?

That's been a long and intense blast of insight, and so we are well overdue some self-exploration.
I know you've been just waiting for that!

In your own teens, how well informed/prepared were you by your parents for navigating sexuality?
(4 means very well.)

0   1   2   3   4

What was the main message you received from this parental input?

_____

_____

How good or helpful was the sex education you received at school (if there was any)?

0   1   2   3   4

What was the main message you received from sex education at school?

_____

Were your early sexual experiences happy ones?

0   1   2   3   4

Have things improved – do you enjoy your sexuality now?

0   1   2   3   4

What, if anything, is keeping you from putting a 4 for that last question?

_____

Would you be comfortable in letting your daughter know that sex can be great?

_____

Once again, sending you a warm hug if that has been a difficult page to fill in. Very many mothers or fathers experience a lot of pain and wounding around their sexual lives, right into the present day. And of course, if we don't feel very good about our own sexual happiness, then it will be hard to convey a good feeling to our girls. But it's important to keep working on this.

We deserve it, and of course they deserve it too. Even if we can be honest and say: 'I am not there yet.' For girls of fourteen and older, this kind of honesty, especially between mother and daughter, is precious and will greatly deepen your relationship. It may not be right to tell her everything about your life, but giving her a broad brush picture will mean it's not all murky and contradictory. Often in families, we sort of know things, but we are not sure if we are allowed to know that we know. It's a huge relief to clear that up.

ELIZABETH CLARK; L.P.C.

Elizabeth is a counsellor specializing in high-need teenagers referred from courts and welfare agencies. Her books include *Parenting Plugged-In Teens: Becoming Their GPS in a Cyber-Sexual World* and *Molly Top's Teen Guide to Love, Sex, and No Regrets*. Elizabeth speaks across the United States on issues relating to young people and the internet. She believes that this generation have enormous benefits and advantages from the connection that cyberspace provides, as long as we guide them towards what is happy and wise.

HOW TO HELP YOUR TEEN STAY HAPPY AND IN CHARGE

The very best sex educator in the world, in my opinion, is a counsellor in a little town called Grand Junction, high in the mountains of Colorado. Elizabeth Clark, and her book, *Molly Top's Teen Guide to Love, Sex, and No Regrets*, manages to be funny, sexy, intelligent and subtle yet very clear, all at the same time. It really wants kids to get the most out of intimacy by not rushing past the places where it occurs.

Elizabeth is especially interested in what to do as a parent during the sexual awakening years, which she describes as a Porsche in the driveway, engine running. *You just really want to drive it.*

Elizabeth points out that even fifty years ago only about 5 per cent of couples waited to be married before they, you know, had sex. And since the 1960s the age of marriage has gone from eighteen to twenty-eight. So really, you have to be joking. Young people are going to do it. Some at twenty-five, some at eighteen, some, tragically, at twelve. And we have to know about that and help them deal with it.

Elizabeth gives some very clear guidelines about what to do. I will try and sum them up here (but buy her books! She does it so much better). Here she talks about how our girls' world differs from ours.

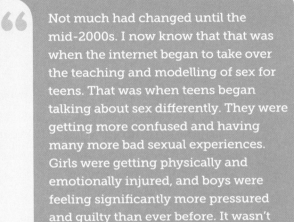

> Not much had changed until the mid-2000s. I now know that that was when the internet began to take over the teaching and modelling of sex for teens. That was when teens began talking about sex differently. They were getting more confused and having many more bad sexual experiences. Girls were getting physically and emotionally injured, and boys were feeling significantly more pressured and guilty than ever before. It wasn't that more teens were having sex. It was the quality, having gone from awkward, to almost abusive.

Elizabeth saw this in perspective – that a lot of other things were going better for teens. They were more confident, better communicators, more engaged with each other, they thought well and quickly. The internet had its plusses. But 'the changing sexual climate overpowered and darkened those positive changes'.

So whose job is it to change this? Elizabeth is convinced it has to be a parent's job. 'Parents have rarely talked directly and honestly with their teens about sex, yet we live in a time when we can no longer follow this precedent.'

How It's Done

What Elizabeth says is to start gentle. Of course, it helps to have talked on and off about sex and reproduction, and love and affection, all through your children's lives in an age-appropriate way. That weird idea about the 'big talk' that our parents and we so dreaded was a terrible way to do things. Sex is part of life. Kids see animals giving birth, and mating, and probably in the playground they are given weird and distorted ideas about it, including of course now, being shown yucky images by wild-eyed kids on their phones or laptops. So we really do have to be in the discussion, and it can be done naturally and in an ongoing way, rather than with any great drama.

And here is the surprising thing – *they want us to.* Elizabeth writes:

> Surveys of teens say they wish their parents would talk to them more about sex. Really. With all their access to everything sexual, why would they care what you had to say? Because most of the stuff they are hearing from movies and TV and porn are fantasies being sold to them as truths, and when they try and emulate these fantasies in real life, they are terribly disappointed and often injured by the experience. Most of them cannot put words to this. Most of them believe that this is as good as it gets. Most of them silently think something is wrong with them because they are terrified or simply not enjoying it. I have known many barely eighteen-year-old girls who apathetically say that they are finished with sexuality.

They want to talk to us. They find it hard. We have to help them. But Elizabeth advises going in slow steps. First of all, create an opening. Ask them, as casually as you can: 'So what is going on in your love life?' This is a more respectful term to use than 'sex life'. It covers everything from a distant crush to a few kisses, to actual sex. Because sexuality is everything along the way.

They will say nothing, or smile, or look annoyed that you have asked. That's OK.

Then: 'Are you talking to anyone online?' Anything could happen here – a name, a gasp, more annoyance, but it doesn't matter, because now they know that you know, and that's all right.

You have five seconds now before they 'close the door', so you say one last thing: 'Listen, I know there is some good stuff and some awful stuff on the internet. I know if I was your age now I'd be curious and having a look. But there's some messed up stuff there too.'

Three seconds to shut down. 'I'd like to start talking with you about that sometime.' And then you drop it!

They know you know. They know you care. They know you will come back to it. And you do. But just in snippets. You don't overload them. Perhaps you watch movies or television and talk about the sexuality portrayed, good and bad. Perhaps you just talk some more as you are going somewhere in the car. You listen and ask questions when they tell you about their friends' lives. You discuss the media's bombardment of sexual images, ask how it makes them feel to see women on ads portrayed as so hot, so sexy, all the time. You can give them good books. Look at websites together. Send them emails with thoughts or things you have read.

What matters is that you get sex into something that is thought about, talked about. When they have words for it, they have choice, they can think. It's not about laying down rules. It's about saying: 'This is sensitive, this is important. I understand it's tricky. It is for everyone. You are in charge. You can choose what you want that is right for you.'

And Talk About Porn

You can also talk about porn. These clear insights from Elizabeth will really help. Show them this list. Ask if this fits with what they might have seen. And be really clear with them – these are myths, and real sex, happy sex, isn't like this:

The Six Myths of Porn

1. **Sex is anonymous.** It doesn't matter if you are attracted to the other person or them to you. It is best if the person is not real to you, has no feelings, family, cares, soul, future or physical limits.

2. **Sex is fast.** There is no kissing or caressing, no unfolding, no allowing arousal to get the body ready.

3. **Sex is disconnected.** No eyes meet. Bodies are not usually positioned facing one another. There are no smiles or moments when soul meets soul, friend meets friend, lover meets lover. Because it doesn't matter who is entering you.

4. **Women love degradation.** They are pummelled, slapped and choked, they are mocked and discarded. They are assumed stupid and without worth. But the important message of porn is that this does not matter because women love this degradation and abuse. It turns them on. It is all part of the fun. (It's almost never the man who is hurt or humiliated – why is that?)

5. **Women are always ready.** Sexy girls are always ready for sex, anytime, anywhere, with anyone and in any way. They just want sex all the time. Their bodies require no time or touch, and no relationship.

6. **Porn sex is a blast**. At the end of the film everyone has had a great time. Everyone is happy, satisfied and content.

Girls do watch porn too, though nowhere near as much as boys (though sometimes girls exposed to porn at a young age become addicted to it, according to some studies and accounts). But mostly girls see when they watch that the actors are faking it, especially the women – as they pretend it's all going great. But not the boys, *they think that's how it goes*. 'Get 'er done', as Elizabeth puts it.

The result, Elizabeth points out, is awful sex. The research tells us this. Less than a fifth of girls have orgasms in the 'hook up' world of teen sex. It's sloppy, unsatisfying and humiliating – even for the boys. Girls in college who are sexually active with more than one partner a year experience high levels of clinical depression. They go together. If we don't help them get clear on this, then porn will wreck their sex lives. And since sex is supposed to be an intense, energizing and bonding part of our lives, that's a huge loss.

Sexting

Talk to them about sexting. Your daughter is likely to come under pressure, sooner or later, from boys wanting her to send photos of herself naked, or near as. This can make a girl feel excited, special, wanted. Or worried. Or a mixture of the two. As Elizabeth writes, boys won't give up:

The boys ask again, and again and again and again. They act adorable. They act hurt by the rejections. They promise love and devotion. They promise not to show anyone. They get mean. They threaten. They are relentless.

About a third of girls eventually send a photo. They almost always instantly regret it. And it's out there. A boy might brag with it to his friends. Use it to pressure her for more. Use it to blackmail or humiliate her if they break up, for revenge. It's a risky thing to do. Sexting is a part of teenage courtship now, but it's still not a great idea. You have to talk to your girl about this – even if she chooses to go ahead, you'll still talk to her, still help her, and she can find out what is best for her.

Elizabeth says so much more in her books. But she always recommends light, casual conversations, and lots of them. No big intense hit. No moralizing. Always a focus on thinking through what is right for you. Always keeping the door open. Being good-humoured and friendly. Kids are afraid of judgement. They are especially afraid we will take away their devices. It's OK to

limit these – for instance, not having Wifi running all night or no devices allowed in bedrooms after a certain time, so they can drop it all and relax. But negotiate what is reasonable. Don't punish them for their honesty.

My favourite paragraph of Elizabeth's is:

You can tell them what real sexuality is like. Tell them that we do much better if we know the other person, if we slowly unfold to sexuality. Tell them if they go slowly they will be safer and healthier and happier. Tell them about all the fun steps from a kiss to intercourse, the steps missed completely by porn. Tell them you hope they play on first and second base, because they are great places to hang around and enjoy, as you really learn to love and trust each other.

RESPECT IS THE KEY

While we have to tackle the specifics, there is a bigger picture that good sex is built on. In the end it's all about respect. Being able to talk about things and listen to each other is only going to happen when you feel emotionally safe. If your girl grows up feeling respected, and seeing others respected, then she will carry that into relationships as well.

How respectful is your household? (A 4 means 'totally agree'.)

1. Dad treats Mum with respect.

    0   1   2   3   4

2. Mum treats Dad with respect.

    0   1   2   3   4

3. People are loving and warm to each other.

    0   1   2   3   4

4. There are no put downs in the way people talk to each other.

    0   1   2   3   4

5. There is no fat-shaming or judging of bodies.

    0   1   2   3   4

6. Brothers treat sisters with respect.

    0   1   2   3   4

7. Sisters treat brothers with respect.

    0   1   2   3   4

8. When you see people out in the world, you talk about them with respect, and don't make put-down comments even among yourselves.

     0   1   2   3   4

9. You don't watch or allow violent or degrading treatment of people on the television or videos or computer games that you watch or play as a family.

     0   1   2   3   4

10. You keep lines of communication open, so that things can be talked about and people aren't afraid to bring up a worry, or ask about something embarrassing.

     0   1   2   3   4

Now – total your scores to obtain your family's Respect Quotient.

_____

If you had a total **30–40**, you are doing great. Well done!

20–30: You could be doing great, but need to target those points that were 2 or less. Go back and circle those.

10–20: In the danger zone, but it's not unusual for families to score this low. Please do begin to make changes. Your family may be under a lot of stress that is causing this, so look into this as well. You have to work as a team, and not undermine each other.

0–10: That sounds like a pretty hard family to feel good in. Even if you are used to it, it's not good for children to be around that much negativity or criticism. It might be a good idea to get professional help, or do a parenting course or seek relationship help. If violence is a risk, it's essential that you seek help. You all deserve and need to be in a better place.

Respect for each other's ideas and points of view, each other's bodies, each other's innate worth as human beings, however flawed, is simply the keystone of all life. Treat others with respect, even if they don't always deserve it. And respect yourself. Then happy sexuality is guaranteed.

A
Happy
Sexuality

In a Nutshell

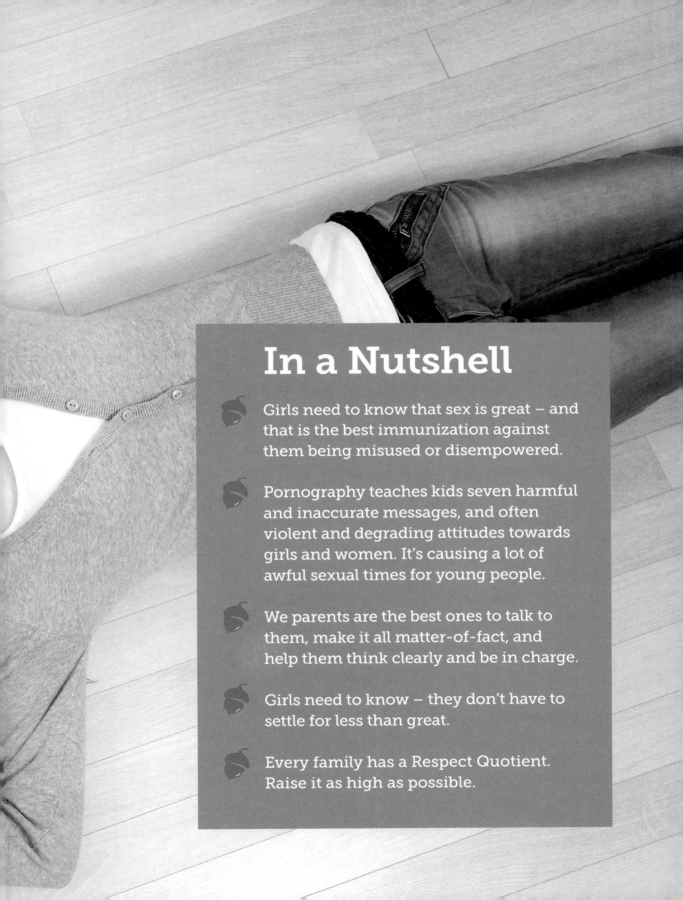

- Girls need to know that sex is great — and that is the best immunization against them being misused or disempowered.

- Pornography teaches kids seven harmful and inaccurate messages, and often violent and degrading attitudes towards girls and women. It's causing a lot of awful sexual times for young people.

- We parents are the best ones to talk to them, make it all matter-of-fact, and help them think clearly and be in charge.

- Girls need to know — they don't have to settle for less than great.

- Every family has a Respect Quotient. Raise it as high as possible.

Chapter Eight

Backbone

> " There is no doubt about it. To live in this world, a girl has to be strong. But how can we pass on this quality? Where does inner strength come from? "

Two of the people I love most in the world are a couple about my age, who, like me, raised two children in rural Australia. When Cheryl was thirty-two she contracted multiple sclerosis, and by the time her kids were in their early teens, she was already in a wheelchair. The family adapted – only able to do half their usual activities on weekends, with only one driver. They got by on one income, despite lots of extra expenses. Each teenager cooked a meal each week for the family. Lisa, at thirteen, managed a different recipe every week. Aaron, fifteen, always made spaghetti bolognese!

Both kids made long commutes to their schools and universities, and had part-time jobs to help with costs. Lisa is now a human rights lawyer working in Haiti. She knows how to stick up for herself. Aaron is an air force engineer. Cheryl's condition progressed: she is now quadriplegic and each day is very hard, though she is secure in her husband and family's love. The kids – and grandkids – skype from across the world every couple of days. Life is still good.

If you boil it down, human character comes down to just two things. Backbone and heart. That's what makes a wonderful person. They are kind and caring – but they are also reliable, enduring and true to their word. It has to be both – backbone without heart just leads to brutality. But heart without backbone is no use in a tight spot – everyone knows someone who is full of caring talk, but just can't be relied on.

Life needs us to be strong and brave, but not in the way most people think. Real strength is on the inside. It's keeping on going when you are dead tired and every fibre of you wants to just give up. It's knowing what is right, and sticking with it even if others criticize you. It's a small girl telling some bullies to leave her friend alone, even though they are much bigger than her and she is totally outnumbered.

Strength is exactly what you'd want in a friend, a partner, or a parent – 'You can count on Margie – if she said she'd be here, she will.' 'Nobody messes with Ange – she may be small but she speaks her mind.' 'Dolores is gentle, but she's incredibly determined. She won't do it if it isn't right.'

In this chapter you'll learn how to give your daughter backbone. And help her to be someone to be very proud of.

But first, here's a quick self-assessment:

How strong do you think you are?

☐   NOT AT ALL

☐   SOMEWHAT

☐   FAIRLY STRONG

☐   CAST IRON

Have you got stronger over the course of your life?

☐   NOT AT ALL

☐   SOMEWHAT

☐   VERY MUCH SO

Write the name of a friend or family member you would describe as strong:

_____

Do they have heart as well? (No need to write that!)

WHAT MAKES GIRLS STRONG?

Well, to begin with, they mostly just are! When they are small we respect that they have wishes and wants – to explore, get our attention, play and do things. This is their natural life force at work, saying: 'Out of my way – let me learn!' They are self-educating little machines, and that means they power into everything.

Of course, we have to stop them putting the kitten into the toilet, or running with scissors. It's not about letting a toddler do everything they want, or giving in to their tantrums. But still, if a little girl finds that she can want things, go after them and get them, then her natural spirit isn't blocked by over-grumpy parents. She can recover from getting stopped sometimes, and not be crushed.

> Long ago, in my very first year as a psychologist, I worked in schools. A small boy was having trouble with learning problems and I was asked to visit his mum, who refused to come into the school. She warily invited me in and we had a cup of tea. A toddler girl sat on the kitchen floor. There were no toys that I could see. Absolutely nothing to play with or do. Every now and then, the toddler would attempt to get into the cupboard where the saucepans were. Her mum walked across, scolded her, slammed the cupboard door, pulled her away, and kept talking to me.

We don't yell, scowl, or overreact to our girls' natural need to learn. We are friendly even as we divert them. We try not to discourage them. (Discourage is an interesting word – isn't it? The taking away of courage!)

When we have to thwart their will, it helps if we explain. Not in great detail, and not expecting it to make a shred of difference right now – when an under-six wants something, they just want it. But giving at least that respect – it's not because you are bad.

FEEL THE FEAR, BUT DO IT ANYWAY

A big part of being strong means being in charge of your emotions. This has two parts to it – first, to be aware of one's emotions (this is part of what is called mindfulness). A strong person has feelings, and can draw on the power of anger, grief or fear, but also knows when these emotions are just getting in the way. She listens to her feelings, but isn't in their grip. So she feels her anger, or fear, or sorrow, or exhaustion, or boredom, acknowledges them, but then moves beyond those and does what she thinks is right anyway.

When girls are older, we explain to them how we ourselves go about doing tough things. Especially, that feeling bad doesn't help. Again, do it gently, it's not: 'bad luck, kid, the world sucks – get used to it', because that either crushes them or sparks rebellion. (Rebellion is a kind of strength, but it's very limiting – you end up shouting at road signs!) The job goes quicker if you don't whinge or whine – even inside your own head.

This is true even in really tough situations – trauma or tragedy. We humans have a unique facility to defer feelings – it's even part of our adrenaline chemistry. We cope at a road accident, rushing a toddler to hospital, getting through a nasty confrontation with someone. And later on we shiver, shake and cry, we let our feelings out. And that's how our mental health is restored.

So explain to your daughter: 'I hate cleaning up after a party! There is just so much mess! But heck, it was a good party. No point being in a bad mood. Let's roll up our sleeves and get it done!'

You teach her about ATTITUDE – which combines the kind of self-talk, and a physical and emotional stance you decide to take. Strength is an attitude. And your daughter needs to study that, understand it and see it in action.

(It's interesting how we view 'strength' in gender terms – the word 'feisty' is one of my favourite words, but it's a word almost always only applied to women and girls. As if someone with sparky defiant attitude and grit is an exception in a female and it needs its own special name.)

The Continuum Concept author Jean Liedloff described the same strength and attitude in her book about the rainforest people of the Amazon. A wooden canoe, heavy, slippery and wet, had almost been dragged to the top of the rapids. It had taken several hours, with many stumbles. Right at the top, a man fell, the canoe bashed into another two and crashed back down several hundred feet to the bottom. The men, without exception, found this hilarious! They sat, ate some food and teased the man who had caused it and the other two with bruised thighs and legs. Then climbed back to the foot of the rapids and started again.

I once shared a farmhouse with a nursing sister. A pet goat had escaped, strayed into dense blackberries and had become entangled. We'd heard its bleating cries of distress. It was pitch dark, windy, and sleety rain was falling. I held the torch for my friend as we tunnelled in through the blackberry canes, cutting and picking our way, and she worked patiently cutting and separating the matted hair of the struggling goat. She never swore, never got angry with the goat, or the brambles. Because it wouldn't have helped.

WHY ROLE MODELS ARE IMPORTANT

In the end, nothing beats your daughter seeing you and other women (and men) doing things bravely. We know from neuroscience that our brains use 'mirror neurons' to take on board the way other people do things – everything our conscious brain would not notice – how they jut their chin, how they plant their legs, how they pitch their voice, how they glare with their eyes, to get just that right amount of 'fear striking' into dealing with, say, poor treatment in a shop, or a creepy man on a crowded train.

Once a girl sees how this is done, it becomes easier, in fact almost second nature. When she is older you can talk about someone who is tough and no-nonsense in her circle of family and friends, someone that she might want to 'channel' when needed.

The aim is to create a girl who is not overbearing or mean, or likely to provoke aggression through having a prickly nature, but who comes across as making sense, having force of personality, and using thinking to work out what is best.

WHY GIRLS NEED ANGER

There's a deeper story with girls and strength. The emotion that helps us most to defend ourselves, or what we think is just and right, is of course anger. No prizes for guessing that. And very often in the past girls were taught, not to put too fine a point on it, to swallow their anger. Men got angry, women muttered and grumbled, but it was male emotions that ruled the house. (Of course not every house – sometimes it was completely the reverse.)

But it's important to know that you can't always be nice and be strong, or at least not easily. The crime and assault research shows that assailants or criminals tend to notice and pick out the quiet looking people for their victims. But even in dealing with some dodgy work on your house, or a rude or intrusive person, it's important to have some rage on hand. And if need be, to show it.

If your daughter isn't good at that, practise with her. Stand a few feet away from each other, take a deep breath, and speak softly, and over the top of each other. Then go louder, then louder still. Choose something for her to shout – NO, I WON'T is a good one. You can then shout YES, YOU WILL to add some heat to the exercise. Relax your throats, breathe deep, and give it all you've got. Build up to full strength shouting, then go down again to a softer level. Try and speak your opposing sentences at the same time.

It's possible that you grew up in a family where anger was dangerous. So you may find it scary at first to be loud. Laugh and bit, loosen up, have a hug. Then practise some more.

BEING FIRM WITH KIDS HELPS THEM BE STRONG

Part of what helps kids develop backbone is the fact that we show backbone with them.

Setting boundaries on behaviour, especially when done in a clear, reasoned way, actually helps our daughters to put the brakes on themselves when they need to – and on other people. Having that language in their vocabulary is very helpful.

Be careful not to press the rebellion button – the second you use accusing, angry or 'because I say so'

language, a part of your daughter will spring up and think (or even say) 'get stuffed!' Make your boundary setting, requests for help around the house and directions of what to do, friendly, with explanations if needed, as if you were talking to a sensible adult. But still make them firm.

It's absolutely OK – and in fact essential – to monitor and keep a check on your daughter (or son) well into their teens. Remember that kids' brains are still very unformed even at sixteen or seventeen and they will make bad choices sometimes if you aren't in there helping work things out, with safety, accountability, curfews and so on. There are bad choices you can learn from, but there are also bad choices that ruin your life.

So, what does monitoring mean?

> When I was barely out of my teens myself, I helped run a youth club for mid-teen kids at our local community centre. When the night was over, some kids would race off, some would be picked up by parents, and some would just hang around as long as they could. I asked a tough-looking girl of about fourteen who was still sitting outside on the steps smoking a cigarette as we packed up to leave: 'Won't your folks be worried where you are?' She replied: 'They don't care.'

Monitoring our kids is caring. Elizabeth Clark, in *Parenting Plugged-In Teens*, recommends the four W's – four questions that you must always ask whenever your child requests to go places and do things. 'What, when, where and who with?' should become so routine that they automatically come to you with answers prepared – from eight to eighteen!

But it doesn't stop there. Every teenager worth their salt will at some stage try to get around you. They will not be where they said, or with whom they said. And your job is to bust them! Elizabeth says that one or two serious busts are usually all you need for a good adolescence – though some kids need more, and others need almost no monitoring at all. An intuition, or something just so improbable that they have promised you, will tip you off, and a phone call will reveal they are not where or doing what they said. Get them home, get them sitting down and you standing up and let them know that lying is a terrible thing to do. You wouldn't do it to them. And they should be ashamed. Some trust rebuilding is going to be needed.

Elizabeth takes a playful approach. While sounding grim and dire, the truth is that it's good to catch a kid out and remind them that they are a kid and you are an adult. As always, don't lose your cool. Be clear, be chilly, but only for a day or two. Long-term, it's about a caring relationship, and your teen needs to know you care about their being safe and happy, or even safe and unhappy. The truth is, bad stuff happens to teens every day, most of which doesn't make it to the newspapers but is still frightening and dangerous. And that's why you do it.

SHARING THE LOAD – A PRACTICE GROUND FOR BEING GROWN UP

There's just space here for a small but very important point. All through history, kids have worked. We are the first society ever to treat our kids like little kings and queens, waited on and provided for. And that creates dependence and weakness. It's totally essential that boys and girls (equally!) share in housework, cleaning, cooking, sorting and shopping, from as young an age as is safe to do so. We infantilize our children (especially teenagers) when we run around after them. And if it's mum who does most of this, that sends a bad message too.

Helping with the family's needs is the ideal practice ground for all those character-building traits – persistence, good humour, co-operation. Even with study to do, they should still help you as well. Do it together and make it a sociable thing.

PUT-DOWN PARENTS – HOW PUT-DOWNS CAN HARM GIRLS' CONFIDENCE

There is a terrible thing that happens in families, and in fact in human relationships of every kind. It leads to alienated and unhappy children, broken marriages and conflict of every kind.

When people are uptight or anxious, angry or dismayed, they often default to put-downs as their stopgap reaction. We have learned not to hit members of our family, as happened in the past. But we haven't stopped hitting them with words. Because this was done to us as kids, we naturally do it to our own. Some fathers are especially prone to this if they learned it from damaged fathers. It was a family heirloom.

If you put your daughter down, she will feel she is no good. She will either lack confidence, or get so rebellious that she will do stupid things just to get back at you. And, worst of all, she will think that's what love is, and marry someone who puts her down as well. If you are a dad, you have to stop using put-downs.

Now, the incredible thing is it's not hard to change. It starts with an honest self-evaluation.

When you were a kid, did your parents hit you or belt you?

☐ OFTEN ☐ SOMETIMES ☐ NEVER

Did your parents yell at you in an angry critical way that was scary?

☐ OFTEN ☐ SOMETIMES ☐ NEVER

Did your parents physically attack you in a rage so that you were scared of being hurt?

☐ OFTEN ☐ SOMETIMES ☐ NEVER

Did your parents verbally attack you using put-downs, swearing, sarcasm or strong expressions like 'useless', 'no good', 'waste of space' or similar?

☐ OFTEN ☐ SOMETIMES ☐ NEVER

If you answered OFTEN for more than one of those, then your childhood was an unsafe one. Your parents were not coping well, and it was way too stressful. And you are going to have to make a really strong commitment not to be like that. A big hug to you for surviving that horrible time, and being a loving dad or mum who wants to do better. And for reading this book.

Here is the best commitment wording:

> I commit to never hit or hurt my girl physically. To never frighten or intimidate her by loud words, or looking like I'm about to hit her or threatening to hurt her. To stop, as best I can, using put-downs and criticisms as a way of sorting out conflict.

Have a real think about it. And if you are ready to make that commitment, then circle that paragraph.

SO WHAT TO DO INSTEAD?

The biggest breakthrough in human relationships was 'invented' by Dr Thomas Gordon in the 1960s, though of course good people had always done this instinctively. But Tom Gordon made it clear and easy, and gave it a name – the I-message.

When parents get angry at kids, their most frequent response is to start sentences with 'you'. 'You are so lazy. You idiot. You get over here. You listen to what I am gonna tell you.'

Now, the thing is, whenever we do that – it usually goes with a pointing finger, which is a dead giveaway – we are basically attacking the person because we are telling them who they are. And nobody reacts well to that. You can frighten a child into behaving for years and years, but they will most likely build up an accumulated dislike for you, and one day show it in one of two ways:

1. **By doing exactly the opposite of what you want. And they will do that just out of anger at you.**
2. **They will one day strike straight back at you directly. (This is more of a boy way to react.)**

> One of my closest friends had a dad who belted her and belittled her and her four sisters all the time. Her mother found five girls hard to manage, and often asked her dad to deal with them, and this was the only way he knew. At about the age of five, my friend felt that she wanted to die. But then she decided that she would live, for one purpose. To grow big and strong enough one day to kill her father. This idea kept her alive. By her late teens, she realized that it would not be a great thing for her to be a murderer, and it would be a lose-lose situation. So she didn't kill him when she had the strength and means to do it. But that was how strongly she felt.

Putting your kids down makes them hate you.

So, what is an I-message?

It's like this. Instead of saying 'You', you say 'I'.

I feel _____ when you _____

because _____

and I would like you to change.

'But that would make me weak!' Not weak. It takes strength to be honest, and clear, and not rely on physical strength or loudness to dominate. Those are the tools of a weak person. Weak, no, but vulnerable, yes.

Vulnerability is the newest discovery in making men especially happy and free. If you open your heart, then strangely, it makes things go better. It's a strong thing to do. For example:

I was scared something had happened to you when you came home an hour later than you promised. I would like to talk to you about what happened, and how you can keep your agreements about coming in. To let you go out at night I need to be able to trust you.

Mum

I am sad that you didn't do the cleaning up, which is your job, because we had a big mess to clean up when we came home. I was counting on you to do your part. It felt like you didn't care about us.

Dad

Backbone

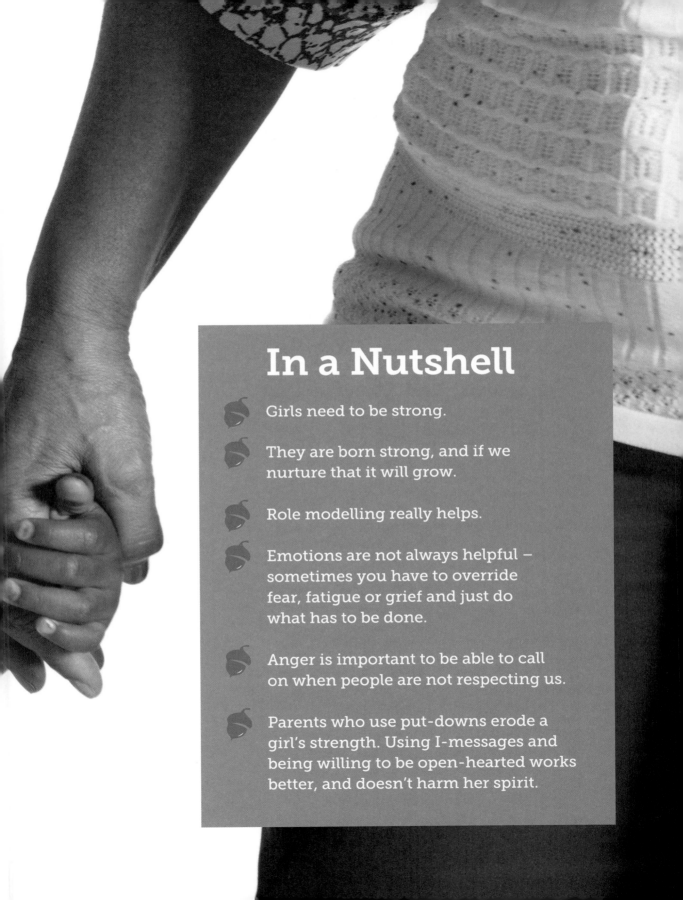

In a Nutshell

- Girls need to be strong.

- They are born strong, and if we nurture that it will grow.

- Role modelling really helps.

- Emotions are not always helpful – sometimes you have to override fear, fatigue or grief and just do what has to be done.

- Anger is important to be able to call on when people are not respecting us.

- Parents who use put-downs erode a girl's strength. Using I-messages and being willing to be open-hearted works better, and doesn't harm her spirit.

Chapter Nine

Feminism

> " Sometimes I go about in pity
> for myself, and all the while, a great
> wind carries me across the sky. "

The school library was almost empty – it was the end of the day and most kids had already left. Through the window Donna could just make out one girl, about thirteen, sitting at a table, and two senior boys standing some distance behind her. She knew the girl slightly – shy, studious, with a friendly nervous smile. She walked towards the entry door and turned to go in, as she had some time before her ride came and it was too cold to wait in the open air.

As she swung through the doorway, she was taken aback that the scene had changed. One of the boys was standing right behind Eloise's chair – she remembered her name now – and reaching his arms around and pinioning her, was grabbing her chest with both hands. The kid looked terror-stricken, white, unable to move or fight him off. The boy spoke in a leering voice: 'No tits there yet?', ruffled the girl's shirt and pulled his arms away. He gave a grin to his laughing mate, and the two brushed past and were gone.

Donna stood rooted to the spot. She knew these boys, and had never liked them. They were prefects. They had surnames that were part of the school history. They could do no wrong. She bent low, and spoke softly to the girl. Then stood up, and walked out of the room. The boys were by the gate, waiting to be picked up. She forced herself to slow her walk, ambled over to them, as if nothing had happened, just waiting like any other day. The bigger one turned to face her. She was as tall as him, she caught his eye. And swung her fist low and hard into his stomach, doubling him over. Actually, she didn't do that, but it was a great thought. She looked him in the eye, and said, 'You might want to tell your parents what you did – they'll be getting a call from the school sometime tonight.' And then she spun on her heels, and went to find the teacher she trusted the most.

This is a short chapter, with a single powerful point. But it will make all the difference. Let's begin with a kick-off self-assessment.

When you hear the word feminism – right now, how do you feel?

☐ **1.** Stirred and positive.

☐ **2.** Complicated feelings.

☐ **3.** Negative.

The aim of this chapter is to get you, and then your daughter, to be able to answer with a 1. It's all for one and one for all in making an equal world.

First, the definition. Whatever you may have read, heard or thought, feminism is a very simple thing. It's the movement to give girls and women the same opportunities as boys and men. If you believe that your daughter should have the same rights, safeties and chances in life as your son, or anyone else's son, you are a feminist.

Lots of baggage has been heaped on. Like any human movement, it's been hijacked, watered down, misrepresented, confused and misused, but those are just peripheral flurries in a wide, strong river of change.

When a maths teacher tells a girl: 'You are good at this, you could be an engineer', that's feminism. When a group of women organize on social media to petition to close down a magazine which is degrading to women (as they did with the Bauer Group's *Zoo Weekly* just last year), or name a politician or sports person who misuses women, as happens almost every week, that's feminism. That your daughter has as much chance of being a doctor, and your son of being a nurse, that's feminism. If it's just as easy for her to become an apprentice plumber, mechanic, gardener or racing jockey and not be taunted, that's feminism. If one day there is no more rape, family violence or sex trafficking anywhere in the world, that's feminism.

SEEING THAT SHE'S PART OF SOMETHING BIG

It's a very human tendency to get so taken up with the day to day that we forget what is really going on. And that particularly applies to teenagers, for whom a pimple can be a disaster. We must lift our heads up and see the big sky. The big story, what our lives are really about.

For a girl, this is especially true. Because the big story for girls is an amazing one. If your daughter had been born a hundred years ago, her life would have been, to our eyes, terrible. She would only have two life choices – to work as a servant in a richer person's house, or to marry. Those were the only ways to have a roof over her head. Had she married, she could own no property, and she had better choose her husband with a great deal of care, because legally he could beat her, rape her, imprison her in their home, and she could do nothing about that. If she left him, she would be homeless and destitute, and unlikely to ever see her children. Without labour-saving devices like washing machines and vacuum cleaners, housework consumed every waking minute. (She might have had the intellect of a surgeon or a scientist, but scrubbing dishes and floors would have been her lot.)

Women could not vote, and their pay if they did work was half that of men. Never enough to live on. There was no birth control other than abstinence. Childbirth was dangerous. Girls who got pregnant either found dangerous and horrendous backyard abortions or went to live in homes for fallen women to have their babies, who were forcibly snatched away. Then they remained spinsters, damaged goods.

Women did work, in horrible factory jobs where they were often subject to sexual abuse by the men in charge of them, who could throw them out if they did not acquiesce.

Then there was a movement. The twentieth century was the age of movements – the trade union movement, the civil rights movement, the peace movement, the environmental movement

– all were massive outbreaks of common sense, outrage and change. They were made possible only because of modern communications. Newspapers, newsreels, film footage, radio, then television, and the internet. People communicated, got together, rose up, and struggled for change. The women's movement was the biggest of them all. Even compared with the cataclysmic wars and scientific advances, in terms of the actual impact on people's lives, it was the most significant event of the twentieth century. Though of course it is far from over in the twenty-first.

Watch the film *Suffragette*. It's actually too violent and disturbing to show girls until they are about fourteen in my opinion. Yet it all really happened in the streets and homes of London, in places you can still walk and visit. People in power – the patriarchy – don't give it up easily. Women who protested for the right to vote were charged by mounted police on horseback, clubbed to the ground with steel-tipped poles. Arrested, they went on hunger strikes. The authorities force-fed them with rubber tubes, a procedure so dangerous and frightening that it resembled waterboarding today. The horror of the medical staff made to carry it out was one of the turning points in the change of public feeling, and the final victory. We, and our daughters, need to realize that this is very recent history.

Another film to show girls is *Made in Dagenham*, set in the 1960s, a touching and up-close story of how women in a British car factory began the worldwide shift towards equal pay. Your daughter – and you – owe them a thank you. (Even that film I wouldn't show to anyone under twelve.)

Your daughter can live, work, fall in love, get an education, forge a career, be safe in her home, get a loan, travel the world, choose whether to have children or not, birth them safely, because millions of women fought for that on her behalf. She needs to know that.

The epidemic of mental health problems suffered by girls today would be greatly helped if girls could realize that the problem *is not in them, but in the world around them*. And instead of being anxious and depressed, get wildly angry. The thing I want you to get your daughters to understand is: 'You are not alone. The things you suffer when boys mistreat you or men leer at you or you feel excluded from career choices or frightened in crowds, or the pressure to be pretty, unopinionated and thin – those are big problems for all women everywhere. And you need to join the fight.'

Feminism

In a Nutshell

Being a female, meant for thousands of years being seen and treated as inferior, and denied the chance for a full, or even a safe and healthy life.

In the twentieth century women rose up and fought for that to change. There's still some way to go.

Your daughter's own individual problems are very often because of the forces and pressures, abuses and inequities in how the world treats girls.

If she realizes this she can feel a whole lot better about herself, and a whole lot angrier – in a good way – at the world.

While our own girls might be okay, billions of girls and women are not. Wouldn't it be great to involve her along with you in doing something about that.

Chapter Ten

Spirit

> Why are we here? What is my life for? We might have forgotten those questions but our teenagers have not. They want to know what it all means, and they need answers as big as the sky.

As a young child, Professor Aileen Moreton-Robinson was taught bush-tracking skills by her grandfather. For an indigenous Australian girl on Stradbroke Island, this was unusual, as tracking was only ever taught to boys. He must have seen something special in her, and he was right – today, Aileen is a leading Australian academic. Is it possible that what this old man patiently taught her was the key to her success? When she was only three her grandfather rebuked her for stamping thoughtlessly on an ants' nest. He told her – just gently – 'You are worth no more than any living thing, and no less than any living thing.' And that was where her education began.

You or I might have said to this little girl, 'Don't step on those ants – they didn't do anything to you!' Or worse, we might have just ignored her. After all, society often seems to have been built on trashing the natural world. What are a few ants here or there? The subtle difference of an aboriginal elder setting out on a girl's education was that he was literally 'putting her in her place'. And for aboriginal people, place is very important, in the landscape, in the cosmos, in the tribe. This was a culture that lasted for hundreds of thousands of years, in which people were deeply happy and alive. Their astonishing durability was based on being superb at raising their children. 'You matter (or why else would I spend the time on you?) – you matter very much. But no more than those ants!' What a mind-bending idea. When one of the world's most influential women, Irish President and later UN Human Rights Commissioner Mary Robinson, wrote her life story, she called it *Everybody Matters*. That concept – every living thing being connected – is the heart of spirituality, as we will explain. And as you will be able to help your daughter understand.

Spirituality isn't a hobby or an interest which we add on to our lives – a bit of church on Sundays or a Buddha in the garden for a touch of Bali in the backyard (though Bali, of course, is Hindu). Spirituality is a fundamental shift, which young humans either make or don't make, to another level of life. It's an essential – we have to reach it or our lives simply don't work. It's that basic. Your daughter needs to know about this, and more important, experience it. Spirituality is the last, and most important, of the ten things girls need most.

YOUR GIRL IS A SPIRITUAL BEING

It's no accident that women are often more spiritually aware than men. Spirituality is about liberation – being free of the things that make you miserable and afraid. It's the ultimate thing your daughter needs in order to be all that she can be. If you can see the spirituality in your girl (and yes, it is already there) and affirm it and nurture it, it will transform her life.

Spirituality affects us when we don't even know it. Were your daughter to fall on the train tracks, you would leap down there and save her, even if it meant losing your own life. That's saying, she matters more than me. Some people would do that for another person's child. Some spend their lives caring for children dying and in danger in remote parts of the world. We love in ever-expanding circles. On one level, that kind of sacrifice doesn't make sense, and it's certainly not the core message of our 'me-first' society. Spirituality means you start to march to a different drum – it's countercultural. But it's so much what is needed right now for our young people. Just look at how self-obsession hurts our girls: 'I've got a pimple – aaargghhh!' 'He hasn't texted back!' 'I hate my stomach!' Spirituality is the ultimate sense of proportion. You matter a great deal. But really, get a life!

This might daunt you, since we adults often really struggle in this area. Our culture is so spiritually impoverished that it offers little support for those asking 'big picture' questions. We are supposed to be wise and steady for our kids, but we so often just get lost in our own lives. We aim for small goals in life – to stay out of trouble, have a nice house, renovate the bathroom. And our kids look to us with an inner hunger we aren't able to meet.

All the same, hope is not lost. What is sleeping in our young people is also sleeping inside us.

Do you consider yourself to be spiritual? (Circle the option that describes you best.)

YES   SOMEWHAT   NO   I DON'T KNOW WHAT THAT MEANS

At what stage in your life have you felt most alive?

0–5   5–10   10–14   14–18   18–25   25–30   30–40   RIGHT NOW

Where in the world have you felt most at peace?

Who is the person you most admire in your life?

In a word, what is it about them that you admire?

Do you have anything in your life that you would call a spiritual practice?

What is sacred to you?

What would you always make a stand on, and not give in?

The very idea of talking about the sacred freaks some people out. Religion, the regular cultural expression of spirituality, carries some terrible baggage. While organized religion has immeasurably improved the ethics, justice and cohesion of society, it has also been the cause of unspeakable violence and persecution, even genocide. Of course, human beings still do those things when they don't follow any religion, but still, the record has not been good, and many people today are wary of any spiritual pursuit. On the other hand, for those who identify with a faith tradition, there are tools, social supports, a language and practices ready-made to help our youngsters – though no adolescent worth their salt ever takes on board their parents' faith without first testing, and for a time, rejecting it. That's an essential part of the spiritual journey. In fact, it's a pre-requisite. It has to be real, not hand-me-down. Spirituality isn't a destination – it's a way of being open to ever-greater learning. It's never about neat or comforting answers.

PART OF IT ALL

So how do we help our girls to experience that they are part of everything, and precious and important beyond their looks or sexiness, school grades or sporting prowess? How do we unhook them from the external? There are things you can point to and be clear about, when your daughter asks you. First of all a definition: spirituality is everything. It's the everything-added-up in totality. We can't put it into words, because words describe separate things. And things aren't separate. So we have to find other ways to help our kids understand it, or in fact experience it.

Sam Miles, the young woman who edits many of my books, is an unusual person. While still in her teens Sam almost died from cancer. It took many operations and ordeals, and she wasn't expected to live – but she did. It's just possible this taught her some lessons very early that might not have come until much later if at all. Sam puts it like this:

> Many of the things people do for fun – spontaneously and happily – express their spirituality. Surfing is a great example of what spirituality is. It is an action, it is physical (involves the body), it can be social (surfing with like-minded others) and underneath it all is the joy of the body being in nature, of being conscious of the tides and the currents, of marine animals and of the weather itself. It has two meanings, like life: it is a thing you do and it is also the thing that refreshes the soul and releases your spirit. Anything that refreshes the soul could be termed spirituality – some find it in dancing to music, some find it cheering their club on at the footy, some find it walking or running in nature, singing in a choir, volunteering at events or helping their elders.
>
> *Sam*

Everyone has things they do which make them feel more at peace, and more alive and free. And we carry this back into our everyday lives, and it makes them go better. Because spirituality is about everything, it has to apply to everything – it's not shut off in a corner of our lives. We take it with us to bed, to our relationships, to school, to work, in how we do friendship. It's a mistake just to associate it with church on Sunday, or a yoga retreat in Bali, or even spending time meditating each day. Each of those is a good starting point, but it doesn't stop there. If spirituality is real then it has to be in everything we do.

A COMPASS TO STEER BY

Secondly, spirituality is a compass. Consciously or unconsciously, we all have a position about why we are in this world. This is implicit in what you pass on to your children. For example:

- **You think the world is either a competition, or a collaboration.**

- **You think we are either separate, or one.**

- **You think nature is either a resource to be used, or a living thing to be cared for on which we utterly depend.**

- **You think either that life has no meaning, or that life is meaning.**

- **You feel either alone and frightened (and so try to make yourself big and important), or comfortable with yourself, at home in the world and free of fear.**

Most of the values of the society around us are absolutely anti-spiritual. Individualism, consumerism and success through the acquisition of fame and wealth are the values that underpin our economy, and what our governments assume we all want. But this is a rat race that only a few can win. This viewpoint has a direct impact on the mental health of our kids. It terrifies them.

The alternative guiding principle is very different. It says that we are in this world as part of a larger whole. That life is an ongoing creation, a kind of symphony, and we can, with sincere effort, approach a harmony with all the other lives around us. Sure, there is death, harm and loss, but against this there is co-operation of society, love and the rewards from the natural world around us – the oceans, land, sky – which sustain us and in which we are co-stewards in keeping things going.

Raising your daughter is right at the heart of this. You are caring for her and for her future, even after you are gone. You are caring for her children, and their children. But you soon find yourself caring for her friends too, and their parents, and your community, and so it grows.

Girls look at their mothers, aunties, fathers, their mother's friends, the teachers at school. They notice – that person is kind. That person is always calm. That person seems so free and able to be themselves. That person is so unconventional and full of life. They know deep down that's what they want to be like. Our job is to teach them that they can.

The thing then is to become more awake to this. To notice what messages we send, in what we say, and what we do ourselves.

WHAT WE TEACH OUR GIRLS

Read through the pairs of sentences below and, from each pair, tick the one that you would like to pass on to your daughter.

☐ In this life you have to look out for yourself. Nobody else will.

OR

☐ Other people matter. We ought to care for them too.

☐ A good life is one filled with material comforts, luxuries and expensive experiences.

OR

☐ A good life is one where you find meaning and purpose in improving the world around you.

☐ When you are dead, it's all over and you'll soon be forgotten.

OR

☐ When you are dead, other people will remember you and carry you in their hearts.

☐ The world is here for us to use.

OR

☐ We are a part of everything. We are here to care for it all.

HELPING YOUR DAUGHTER'S SPIRITUAL AWAKENING

Small children are naturally spiritual. They feel part of everything. But this sense of spirituality needs help to become established and be carried with them throughout their lives. The welcoming of daughters to adulthood, which we described in Chapter 6, may be essential to this. From a material, non-sacred point of view, when we think of what being adult means, we generally think it means leaving the family to join the procession of job-seeking, rent-paying, family-raising consumer life. This can make growing up sound like a negative. They might receive the message: 'You're on your own, kid.'

But that's not the feeling that your daughter will receive at her initiation from a group of older people gathering round who are saying: 'This is special, you are special.' It's not an ejection out into society, it's a welcoming in to a small tribe which will always be there for her. First, you have to make that tribe.

Indigenous cultures were not pushing their girls out into an uncaring world, but into the community of adults, to an actual team of real women. They are saying: 'We are enlisting you to our adult purpose. And that purpose is no less than the preservation of life. All life. The human community, the animal community, the plant community, the cosmos. We have a sacred role'. You can help your daughter awaken her spirituality, not to mention her life's purpose, in exactly the same way.

Becoming an adult human requires an awakening. Kids know this; they go looking for it. All their travelling, their surfing, their music, their lovemaking, drinking and drug-taking, can be viewed as attempts to discover what they know intuitively is out there and inside themselves. Some of them make it. But a lot don't.

Being a proper adult is a realization. It means you have received or decoded or deduced a simple, but yet very confronting message. You are not in this world for yourself. Embrace life, love it, enjoy it to the full. But remember that we are here for each other. If you miss this message, you run the risk of living life only on the surface. And shrivelling up and dying on the inside.

SO WE COME TO THE END

My final message to you is: 'You can do this'. Let your daughter be free to be herself, to make music, to create art or dance. To investigate the insides of machines, or cells, or people. Take her to see wild waves or to run in the rain on the beach. Then, one day, she might be sitting on a rocky outcrop somewhere, or still beside a stream, or deep in a conversation, and it will hit her. A feeling of peace, and belonging, which is deeper than anything she has ever felt. She will be at home in the universe. And that feeling will not ever leave her.

In this book we have covered ten things that matter most for girls to have happy lives:

- **To be loved and cared for.**

- **To be encouraged to be wild and free.**

- **To be close to others.**

- **To be cherished by a father or father figure.**

- **To find a special passion or interest.**

- **To have wise women who help her become adult.**

- **To have a happy and powerful sexuality.**

- **To learn to be strong.**

- **To be part of the collective effort to set all women free.**

- **And the tenth one is part of all nine that came before. Each one takes us to the heart of life as a human being, as part of the community of all beings, and weaves us into the dance.**

A girl who receives all these amazing blessings vibrates with a happy, connected sense of joy. She is neither crushed by self-consciousness or imprisoned by self-importance. She is delightfully lost in being alive, doing her part and celebrating her moment in the sun. She will have arrived at her true potential.

It's rarely possible that we can give all of these ten things to our girls. Please don't beat yourself up that her childhood hasn't been – and won't be – perfect. That's what we use the word 'grace' for – the fact that somehow life stitches itself into something amazing, as much from the imperfections as from the things that have gone okay.

You love her and you do your best, and over the years of her growing up she comes to realize that. That happy, connected sense of being part of something bigger grows in her like a deep reservoir to draw on. She becomes not just loved, but loving.

Human survival has always been on a knife-edge. Yet so far we have thrived. That's because we have passed on this flame of loving for millions of years. We keep going – our kids keep going – because we know there is a 'more' to life than just the shallow waters of self.

That's why young people get restless and do dumb things, why they keep raging against anything less than holy as a purpose in life. They will not only survive but will go further than us, because we have given them all we can – a start in the world and a resolve to settle for nothing less than wonderful.

And who could ask for more?

Steve Biddulph
Tasmania, 2017

DON'T SETTLE FOR LESS THAN WONDERFUL

Endnotes

p. 12. the Department for Education is reporting…

C. Lessof *et al.*, 'Longitudinal study of young people in England cohort 2: health and wellbeing at wave 2', UK Department for Education research report, July 2016.

p. 12. The NHS says the same…

S. McManus, P. Bebbington, R. Jenkins and T. Brugha (eds), *Mental Health and Wellbeing in England: Adult Psychiatric Morbidity Survey*, Leeds: NHS Digital, 2016.

p. 36. Drug use among teenagers…

D. C. McBride *et al.*, 'Sector health care affairs: quality of parent–child relationship and adolescent HIV risk behavior in St. Maarten', *AIDS Care* 17 (2005), pp. 45–54.

p. 40. This is caused by the neurological meltdown…

D. Siegel, *Brainstorm: The Power and Purpose of the Teenage Brain*, London: Scribe, 2014.

p. 46. They go so far off the rails…

Without clear intervention, risky adolescent life paths tend to worsen or continue into adult life. The main ways that girls and young women cope maladaptively with stress are termed 'internalizing' behaviours (so that they harm or endanger themselves rather than others). These include self-harm or suicidal behaviour, anxiety and depression, eating disorders, risky sexual behaviour, binge drinking and other substance abuse. Some girls also externalize through bullying, violence, theft and other behaviours.

W. Bor *et al.*, 'Are child and adolescent mental health problems increasing in the 21st century? A systematic review', *Australian and New Zealand Journal of Psychiatry* 48 (July 2014), pp. 606–16.

I. Colman *et al.*, 'Forty-year psychiatric outcomes following assessment for internalizing disorder in adolescence', *American Journal of Psychiatry* 164:1 (January 2007), pp. 126–33.

B. Mars *et al.*, 'Clinical and social outcomes of adolescent self-harm: population-based birth cohort study', *British Medical Journal* 349 (2014), g5954.

p. 52. if they are allowed to play free until the age of seven…

Eighty-eight per cent of the world's children begin school at the age of six or seven. Only the UK and former British colonies start school at five or younger. An extensive list of the research evidence for a kindergarten stage as opposed to early school starting is provided at www.upstart.scot/the-evidence.

p. 52. the most anxious girls today are often those…

C. Lessof *et al.*, 'Longitudinal study of young people in England cohort 2: health and wellbeing at wave 2', UK Department for Education research report, July 2016.

p. 53. Our eyes, ears, hands, limbs, feet and, ultimately, our brain need the complex and richly sensory world that only nature can provide…

The scientific case for this, and ways to remedy 'nature-deficit disorder', are comprehensively covered in R. Louv, *Vitamin N: The Essential Guide to a Nature-Rich Life*, New York: Algonquin Books, 2016.

Further reading and citations may be found at childrenandnature.org.

In the UK the leading advocate of returning more nature to children's lives is the commentator and author George Monbiot. See for example www.theguardian.com/commentisfree/2012/nov/19/children-lose-contact-with-nature.

p. 57. It is known from research that dads do more adventurous…

Richard Fletcher at the University of Newcastle, Australia, has carried out extensive research into father–child play and its benefits. His academic papers are numerous, but a summary may be found in his book *The Dad Factor*, Sydney: Finch Publishing, 2011.

There is also a very useful summary of current research in this *Wall Street Journal* article: www.wsj.com/articles/roughhousing-lessons-from-dad-1402444262.

p. 58. Marketers realized there was an untapped demographic…

Comprehensive coverage of commercial targeting of children, with extensive research citations, may be found at www.uow.edu.au/~sharonb/children.html.

p. 59. Those advertisers succeeded beyond their wildest dreams…

N. Micali *et al.*, 'Adolescent eating disorder behaviours and cognitions: gender-specific effects of child, maternal and family risk factors', *British Journal of Psychiatry* 207:4 (2015), pp. 320–7.

p. 59. And one girl in twelve will develop an eating disorder…

The National Eating Disorders Collaboration, *Eating Disorders: The Way Forward: An Australian National Framework*, Sydney: NEDC, 2010.

See also www.eatingdisorders.org.au/key-research-a-statistics.

p. 62. Studies are backing up what teachers are noting with alarm…

J. Dockrell *et al.*, 'Supporting children with speech language and communication needs: an overview of the results of the Better Communication Research Programme', *International Journal of Language and Communication Disorders*. Article first published online, 24 June 2014.
There are also good discussions of this at www.telegraph.co.uk/education/educationnews/11497018/Twice-as-many-boys-as-girls-are-starting-school-unable-to-speak-properly-report.html

and

theconversation.com/were-not-talking-to-our-kids-are-we-causing-speech-delay-23585.

Further coverage of the wider research picture is at www.literacytrust.org.uk/assets/0000/1151/discussionpaper.pdf.

p. 70. psychologist Michael Thompson describes seven key skills that make up friendship competence…

M. Thompson PH.D. and C. O'Neill Grace, *Best Friends, Worst Enemies: Understanding the Social Lives of Children*, New York: Ballantine Books, 2002.

p. 75. some great insights are given about friendship in the under-eights…

Dr M. Anthony M.A. PH.D. and R. Lindert PH.D., *Little Girls Can Be Mean: Four Steps to Bully-Proof Girls in the Early Grades*, New York: St. Martin's Griffin, 2010.

p. 76. Research shows that boys use more physical bullying…

The Ditch the Label Annual Bullying Report for 2016 is available at ditchthelabel.org.

p. 86. For at least 90 per cent of girls…

The difficulties of estimating the extent of same-sex attraction are well explored in www.ncbi.nlm.nih.gov/pmc/articles/PMC2603519, which cites a Canadian survey that 6.4 per cent of sexually active girls had experienced sexual activity with a same-sex partner in the previous year. Being predominantly same-sex attracted could safely be estimated as comprising less than 10 per cent of young people, but the boundaries are far from clear and it might be that sexuality ought not to be categorized at all.

p. 96. Bruce discovered research that families who eat together…

The study linking families having dinner together and reduced levels of drug use in teens attracted a great deal of attention in the early 2010s. However, more thoughtful analysis suggested that families who got on well were more likely to eat together, and closer relationships rather than meals per se were the link to lower levels of drug use in teens. For families with high levels of conflict, eating together could make things worse. Still, the main message holds: there is greater chance of engagement – and oxytocin hormones actually rise when humans eat together – so having family meals is still a very valuable practice.

www.centeronaddiction.org/newsroom/press-releases/2011-family-dinners.

healthland.time.com/2012/06/07/do-family-dinners-really-reduce-teen-drug-use.

p. 112. Peter Benson's team researched the concept…

www.search-institute.org/research/insights-evidence/november-2010.

www.parentfurther.com also has useful resources for parents, including video on talking to your child about spark.

p. 117. Benson found that about half of the young people he studied…

www.search-institute.org/research/insights-evidence/november-2010.

p. 144. A recent study by the Burnet Institute…

M. S. Lim *et al.*, 'The impact of pornography on gender-based violence, sexual health and well-being: what do we know?' *Journal of Epidemiology & Community Health* 70:1 (January 2016), pp. 3–5.

p. 145. One study found that 88 per cent of porn…

A. J. Bridges *et al.*, 'Aggression and sexual behavior in best-selling pornography videos: a content analysis update', *Violence Against Women* 16 (2010), p. 1065.

p. 153. Less than a fifth of girls have orgasms…

Most studies today report that young women barely focus on their own sexual pleasure and concentrate instead on avoiding pain, which 53 per cent experience as part of their sexual interactions with boys. His pleasure and how they 'perform' are the main focus. It's likely that their mothers' generation had more fulfilling sex lives 30 years ago than young women do today.

N. J. Sales, *American Girls: Social Media and the Secret Lives of Teenagers*, New York: Knopf, 2015.

P. Orenstein, *Girls & Sex: Navigating the Complicated New Landscape*, New York: Harper, 2016.

p.165. *The Continuum Concept* author Jean Liedloff described the same strength and attitude in her book about the rainforest people of the Amazon…

J. Liedoff, *The Continuum Concept*, London: Arkana, 1989.

p.170. Tom Gordon made it clear and easy, and gave it a name – the I-message…

Dr T. Gordon, *Parent Effectiveness Training: The Proven Program for Raising Responsible Children, 30th edition*, New York: Three Rivers Press, 2008.

p. 184. It's no accident that women are often more spiritually aware…

A. Desrosiers and L. Miller, 'Relational spirituality and depression in adolescent girls', *Journal of Clinical Psychology* 63:10 (October 2007), pp. 1021–37.

A. N. Bryant, 'Gender differences in spiritual development during the college years, *Sex Roles* 56:11 (June 2007), pp. 835–46.

Further Reading

There are many great books out there, but I have chosen these ones because they push the boundaries, are just wonderful, or take you further along specific areas of interest or concern. They will enrich and help you build on what you have learned here.

Each book is very different, and different ones will appeal to different readers. Check them out online, then visit your local bookshop, and follow your instinct about which will help you the most.

The New Puberty: How to Navigate Early Development in Today's Girls
Louise Greenspan MD and
Julianna Deardoff PhD
Rodale/Macmillan, 2014
There's been a doubling of girls starting puberty before the age of eight. That's an alarming statistic, but this thoughtful and science-rich book helps you avoid the causes in foods, cosmetics and household products that trigger hormonal changes in girls, and manage the psychological care of your girl if she is an 'early maturer'. It's a very important subject, and these well-qualified authors get the balance just right between concern and reassurance that something can be done.

Molly Top's Teen Guide to Love, Sex and No Regrets
Elizabeth L. Clark
Molly Top, 2017
As mentioned in Chapter 7, this is my all-time, stand-alone, best book for teenagers to read. They know the plumbing, what they need is the joy. And permission to go slow. *Parenting Plugged-in Teens* is the twin to this – the parent's book, with that same straight-shooting, funny and incredibly helpful encouragement to know how to set boundaries, give great information and stop scaring yourself to death!

Simplicity Parenting
Kim John Payne
Ballantine Books, 2010
Equally applicable to girls and boys, this book is timely and revolutionary. It's part of a movement to declutter our homes, our children's lives and our families' routines. Essentially it argues that we and our kids now live in a kind of fever of too much input, too much choice, and importantly too little time to settle, integrate, connect or even just enjoy our lives. And for kids this can be very bad, tipping what are just quirks of temperament into full-grown disorders – ADHD, anxiety, OCD, depression, violence, even suicide. Just having fewer toys is a start – it makes it easier to choose and play. But fewer activities, less media, more family chilling out, and a more quiet and visually simple home – the benefits of simplicity restored to family life are enormous. And, given the tendency of so many girls to anxiety, it can be life-saving.

Rites for Girls: Easing Your Daughter's Passage into Womanhood

Kim McCabe

Little, Brown Book Group, 2018

This is the full story of the ideas introduced in Chapter 6, exploring how to create community around your girl and help her really enjoy and treasure the process of becoming a woman. The idea that we can put a whole missing piece back into girlhood that was ancient and vitally important is catching the imagination of mothers all over the world.

Children's Imagination: Creativity Under Our Noses

Ursula Kolbe

Peppinot Press, 2014

Doing and making is the heart of childhood, and it's also the way small children's brains reach their full potential – without misguided attempts to train or teach, but through the joy of creating what comes from the inside. We can help and foster this, sometimes by being involved, and sometimes by staying on the sidelines. With hundreds of great examples of what children make and do, and why it matters, this book sets you up as the nurturer of your child's own powerful self-development through interaction with the world of things around them. This book knocked my socks off, and continues to do so. It changed how I am with children.

Daughters and Their Dads: Tips for Fathers, Adult Daughters, Husbands and Father Figures

Bruce Robinson

Macsis, 2008

Bruce is Australia's premier encourager of dads. This book features dozens of practical tips in plain-speaking dad-language, and examples from dozens of well-known and ordinary fathers and daughters talking about the difference dads can make. It's half inspiration, half how-to, and concrete and clear. It also helps mums to come to understand and value the role that dads can play.

Sparks: How Parents Can Ignite the Hidden Strengths of Teenagers

Peter L. Benson

John Wiley and Sons Ltd, 2008

The full wrap on what we introduced in Chapter 5. The whole concept of finding, nurturing and appreciating the importance of your daughter or son's passionate interests. Also listen to Peter speaking wonderfully about this by googling 'Peter Benson Spark' for his famous TED talk.

Girls Will Be Girls: Raising Confident and Courageous Daughters

JoAnn Deak and Teresa Barker

Hyperion, 2002

JoAnn is the patron saint of girls' education and girls' self-esteem. Where Mary Pipher raised the alarm in her wonderfully perceptive and caring *Reviving Ophelia*, JoAnn Deak sets out to tackle the problem. Also in a companion book for schools, *How Girls Thrive*, Deak writes about how schools, teachers and parents can restore the vitality, confidence and energy of girls, and their willingness to be smart, independent and themselves.

Her Next Chapter
Lori Day and Charlotte Kugler
Chicago Review Press, 2014

Written by a mother-and-daughter team, this book sets out a single idea – of mother-and-daughter book clubs, where women and girls meet regularly to discuss books they have all read. From this base they look at how such clubs can overcome bullying, body-image problems, gender stereotypes and five other major girlhood toxins. Thousands of mothers have been encouraged to start these groups, and the benefits of having other mothers interact with your girl, share their life wisdom (and suffering), and just the fun and bonding on a deep level make it an unforgettable and precious part of helping her through the teen years, staying close and giving her a 'village'. Lori is a noted writer and campaigner for girls' wellbeing in Massachusetts.

I Am an Emotional Creature: The Secret Life of Girls Around the World
Eve Ensler
Random House, 2010

This is a book to reach into your guts. Eve wrote the world-famous, powerful and liberating *The Vagina Monologues* stage play. This collection of thoughts, poems and essays by her and by girls in gritty and real situations stirs, horrifies and mobilizes you – and any teenage girl – to stand up and fight. And cry and rage and grow. Everything awful that can happen, every possible reaction, the whole terrible face of how the world treats girls, and yet not a second is abandoned to victimhood. If you have a daughter, you have to be able to go there. This book will really help.

Best Friend, Worst Enemies: Understanding the Social Lives of Children
Michael Thompson and Catherine O'Neill-Grace
Ballantine Books, 2002

A sensitive and clear understanding of how friendships work in children at each age and stage, and how to get to the bottom of problems so we can really help them – or support them to help themselves. Making and keeping friends is such a vital part of life for us all, and this book helps reduce the pain and increase the chances of having happy relationships for life.

Wild: A Journey from Lost to Found
Cheryl Strayed
Knopf/Random House, 2012

Same title, whole different book. This is the book made into a superb film starring Reese Witherspoon. Abused by her grandfather, then losing her mother to cancer while still in her teens, Cheryl Strayed went off the rails. Addicted to drugs and sex, she had a fierce intelligence and spirit and knew she had to save herself. So she walked one of the world's longest hikes alone. Here, too, the real dangers were human ones. Spiritually and emotionally, healing takes guts. Luckily most of us don't start quite so far back. Strayed has become a world-renowned counsellor and the author of *Tiny Beautiful Things,* which is the best 'advice to the lovelorn' book I ever read. And who isn't lovelorn sometimes!

Picture Credits

A and N Photography/Shutterstock p120; Africa Studio/Shutterstock p106; Alena Ozerova/Shutterstock p127, 169; Andrey Arkusha/Shutterstock p191; areebarbar/Shutterstock p132; Biddiboo/Getty Images p44, 117; Blend Images – Dave & Les Jacobs/Getty Images p47; Blend Images/Shutterstock p99; Chev Wilkinson/Getty Images p136; comodigit/Shutterstock p73; Daniel Tran Photography pp196–7; de Visu/Shutterstock p188; Deborah Jaffe/Getty Images p143; Diego Cervo/Shutterstock pp210–11; Elizabeth Clark p150; Evgeny Atamanenko/Shutterstock pp104–5; Fritz Photography Teens/Alamy Stock Photo p80; Galina Barskaya/Shutterstock p152; Gary John Norman/Getty Images pp82–3; George Rudy/Shutterstock p84, 155; Ghislain & Marie David de Lossy/Getty Images pp64–5; gpointstudio/Shutterstock p124; Gualberto Becerra/Shutterstock p185; Halfpoint/Shutterstock p13; Hogan Imaging/Shutterstock pp172–3; holbox/Shutterstock pp26–7; Joana Lopes/Shutterstock pp138–9; Jose Luis Pelaez Inc/Getty Images p160; junpinzon/Shutterstock p144; Kevin Dodge/Getty Images p87; Lucky Business/Shutterstock p135; Magdalena Frackowiack p129; Mariia Masich/Shutterstock p35; Mat Hayward/Shutterstock pp180–1; Minnikova Mariia/Shutterstock p103; MNStudio/Shutterstock pp118–19; Monkey Business Images/Shutterstock p32, 74; Narikan/Shutterstock p63; Nick David/Getty Images p41; Oleg Mikhaylov/Shutterstock p55; Paul Bradbury/Getty Images p140; pikselstock/Shutterstock pp158–9; Plainpicture/fstop/Antenna p192; Pollar SD/Shutterstock pp90–1; PopTika/Shutterstock p182; Pressmaster/Shutterstock p37; Purcell Pictures, Inc/Alamy Stock Photo p59; Rachel Weill/Getty Images p149; racorn/Shutterstock p101; Rawpixel.com/Shutterstock pp14–15; Renphoto/Getty Images p2; Skip Nall/Getty Images p109; SolStock/Getty Images p66; spass/Shutterstock p69; SpeedKingz/Shutterstock p76, 78; Steve Biddulph p9; StockLite/Shutterstock pp42–3; Syda Productions/Shutterstock p179; Tania Kolinko/Shutterstock p18; Tatyana_K/Shutterstock p50; Tatyana Vyc/Shutterstock p25, 195; Tetra Images/Getty Images p6; Tim Hale Photography/Getty Images p36; Tyler Olson/Shutterstock p38; University of Western Australia p95; vlavetal/Shutterstock p28; Yuganov Konstantin/Shutterstock p167, 174.

Index

Acknowledgements

This book arises from my life and work, neither of which could have happened without the profound help of Shaaron Biddulph, my partner of forty years. Shaaron brings the intelligence and understanding of people to my energy and good intentions. She showed me how to live a life for other people.

Editorial director Carolyn Thorne gave the book enormous amounts of input and encouragement, and Kathy Dyke worked over the details of the text. Kate Elton, executive publisher, got excited about the idea of an interactive book, and it all flowed from there. Wonderful designers and photographers completed the work. The input of international colleagues Bruce Robinson, Elizabeth Clark and Kim McCabe added what I could not offer.

Ariana Biddulph helped with research, and Vanessa Warren and Ramona Biddulph with ideas and inspiration. The many girls and young women, mothers and fathers I encountered as a therapist and educator provided the burning sense of purpose to carry it through.

As I was completing the book, my only sibling, Christine Howard, succumbed to the long-term effects of multiple sclerosis. She was my first friend and a wonderful sister, funny and irreverent, caring and interested as if she had no challenges of her own.